CONVERSATIONS
WITH SCRIPTURE:
THE BOOK
OF JUDGES

Other Books in the Series

CONVERSATIONS
WITH SCRIPTURE:

THE BOOK
OF JUDGES

ROY L. HELLER

Morehouse Publishing
NEW YORK · HARRISBURG · DENVER

Morehouse Publishing, 4775 Linglestown Road, Harrisburg, PA 17112

Morehouse Publishing, 445 Fifth Avenue, New York, NY 10016

Morehouse Publishing is an imprint of Church Publishing Incorporated.

Cover art: "Joshua and the Fall of Jericho," courtesy of Photos.com.

Series cover design by Corey Kent

Series design by Beth Oberholtzer

Library of Congress Cataloging-in-Publication Data

Heller, Roy L., 1963–
     Conversations with scripture : the book of Judges / Roy L. Heller.
          p.   cm. — (Anglican Association of Biblical Scholars study series)
     Includes bibliographical references.
     ISBN 978-0-8192-2756-0 (pbk.)
     ISBN 978-0-8192-2757-7 (e-book)
     1. Bible. O.T. Judges—Criticism, interpretation, etc. I. Title.
BS1305.52.H45   2011
222'.3206—dc23
                                                                                2011017604

Printed in the United States of America

To Barb and Don

Those who are wise among the people will inherit honor,
and their name will live forever.
—Sɪʀᴀᴄʜ 37:26

O God, the Father of all, whose Son commanded us
to love our enemies: Lead them and us from prejudice
to truth: deliver them and us from hatred, cruelty, and
revenge; and in your good time enable us all to stand
reconciled before you, through Jesus Christ our Lord.

AMEN.

Blessed Lord, who caused all holy Scriptures to be written
for our learning: Grant us so to hear them, read, mark,
learn, and inwardly digest them, that we may embrace
and ever hold fast the blessed hope of everlasting life,
which you have given us in our Savior Jesus Christ; who
lives and reigns with you and the Holy Spirit, one God,
for ever and ever.

AMEN.

CONTENTS

INTRODUCTION
TO THE SERIES

To talk about a distinctively Anglican approach to Scripture is a daunting task. Within any one part of the larger church that we call the Anglican Communion there is, on historical grounds alone, an enormous variety. But as the global character of the church becomes apparent in ever-newer ways, the task of accounting for that variety, while naming the characteristics of a distinctive approach becomes increasingly difficult.

In addition, the examination of Scripture is not confined to formal studies of the kind addressed in this series of parish studies written by formally trained biblical scholars. Systematic theologian David Ford, who participated in the Lambeth Conference of 1998, rightly noted that although "most of us have studied the Bible over many years" and "are aware of various academic approaches to it," we have "also lived in it" and "inhabited it, through worship, preaching, teaching and meditation." As such, Ford observes, "The Bible in the Church is like a city we have lived in for a long time." We may not be able to account for the history of every building or the architecture on every street, but we know our way around and it is a source of life to each of us.[1]

That said, we have not done as much as we should in acquainting the inhabitants of that famed city with the architecture that lies within. So, as risky as it may seem, it is important to set out an introduction to the highlights of that city—which this series proposes to explore at length. Perhaps the best way in which to broach that task is to provide a handful of descriptors.

The first of those descriptors that leaps to mind is familiar, basic, and forever debated: *authoritative*. Years ago I was asked by a colleague who belonged to the Evangelical Free Church why someone with as much obvious interest in the Bible would be an Episcopal priest. I responded, "Because we read the whole of Scripture and not just the parts of it that suit us." Scripture has been and continues to play a singular role in the life of the Anglican Communion, but it has rarely been used in the sharply prescriptive fashion that has characterized some traditions.

Some have characterized this approach as an attempt to navigate a *via media* between overbearing control and an absence of accountability. But I think it is far more helpful to describe the tensions not as a matter of steering a course between two different and competing priorities, but as the complex dance necessary to live under a very different, but typically Anglican notion of authority itself. Authority shares the same root as the word "to author" and as such, refers first and foremost, not to the *power* to *control* with all that both of those words suggest, but to the capacity to *author creativity*, with all that both of those words suggest.[2] As such, the function of Scripture is to carve out a creative space in which the work of the Holy Spirit can yield the very kind of fruit associated with its work in the church. The difficulty, of course, is that for that space to be creative, it is also necessary for it to have boundaries, much like the boundaries we establish for other kinds of genuinely creative freedom—the practice of scales for concert pianists, the discipline of work at the barre that frees the ballerina, or the guidance that parents provide for their children. Defined in this way, it is possible to see the boundaries around that creative space as barriers to be eliminated, or as walls that provide protection, but they are neither.

And so the struggle continues with the authority of Scripture. From time to time in the Anglican Communion, it has been and will be treated as a wall that protects us from the complexity of navigating without error the world in which we live. At other times, it will be treated as the ancient remains of a city to be cleared away in favor of a brave new world. But both approaches are rooted, not in the limitations of Scripture, but in our failure to welcome the creative space we have been given.

For that reason, at their best, Anglican approaches to Scripture are also *illuminative*. William Sloane Coffin once observed that the problem with Americans and the Bible is that we read it like a drunk uses a lamppost. We lean on it, we don't use it for illumination.[3] Leaning on Scripture—or having the lamppost taken out completely—are simply two very closely related ways of failing to acknowledge the creative space provided by Scripture. But once the creative space is recognized for what it is, then the importance of reading Scripture illuminatively becomes apparent. Application of the insight Scripture provides into who we are and what we might become is not something that can be prescribed or mapped out in detail. It is only a conversation with Scripture, marked by humility, that can begin to spell out the particulars. Reading Scripture is, then, in the Anglican tradition a delicate and demanding task, that involves both the careful listening for the voice of God and courageous conversation with the world around us.

It is, for that reason, an approach that is also marked by *critical engagement* with the text itself. It is no accident that from 1860 to 1900 the three best-known names in the world of biblical scholarship were Anglican priests, the first two of whom were bishops: B. F. Westcott, J. B. Lightfoot, and F. J. A. Hort. Together the three made contributions to both the church and the critical study of the biblical text that became a defining characteristic of Anglican life.

Of the three, Westcott's contribution, perhaps, best captures the balance. Not only did his work contribute to a critical text of the Greek New Testament that would eventually serve as the basis for the English Revised Version, but as Bishop of Durham he also convened a conference of Christians to discuss the arms race in Europe, founded the Christian Social Union, and mediated the Durham coal strike of 1892.

The English roots of the tradition are not the only, or even the defining characteristic of Anglican approaches to Scripture. The church, no less than the rest of the world, has been forever changed by the process of globalization, which has yielded a rich *diversity* that complements the traditions once identified with the church.

Scripture in Uganda, for example, has been read with an emphasis on private, allegorical, and revivalist applications. The result has been a tradition in large parts of East Africa that stresses the reading of Scripture on one's own; the direct application made to the contemporary situation without reference to the setting of the original text; and the combination of personal testimony with the power of public exhortation.

At the same time, however, globalization has brought that tradition into conversation with people from other parts of the Anglican Communion as the church in Uganda has sought to bring the biblical text to bear on its efforts to address the issues of justice, poverty, war, disease, food shortage, and education. In such a dynamic environment, the only thing that one can say with certainty is that neither the Anglican Communion, nor the churches of East Africa, will ever be the same again.

Authoritative, illuminative, critical, and varied—these are not the labels that one uses to carve out an approach to Scripture that can be predicted with any kind of certainty. Indeed, if the word *dynamic*—just used—is added to the list, perhaps all that one can predict is still more change! And, for that reason, there will be observers who (not without reason) will argue that the single common denominator in this series is that each of the authors also happens to be an Anglican. (There might even be a few who will dispute that!)

But such is the nature of life in any city, including one shaped by the Bible. We influence the shape of its life, but we are also shaped and nurtured by it. And if that city is of God's making, then to force our own design on the streets and buildings around us is to disregard the design that the chief architect has in mind.

—Frederick W. Schmidt
Series Editor

AUTOBIOGRAPHICAL NOTE

I was not born into an Episcopal Church household. For the first twenty-two years of my life, I worshipped at a small Pentecostal church in Baytown, Texas. That grace-filled experience gave me many gifts: a sense of a close and loving community, a deep-seated awareness that God is intimately involved in our lives, and a well-grounded knowledge of the Bible. This last gift, in particular, has been a defining factor in my life; the Bible was not simply something we heard read on Sunday mornings, but was something that we were expected to read every day. Its stories were not only confined to Sunday school classrooms, but were used by us—day by day—to encourage each other toward faithful living. The cadences of its psalms and epistles were not only a part of the songs we sang in church, but also seasoned our everyday speech. Within that community, I had a sense, not that the Bible was a part of my life, but rather that my life was a part of the message of the Bible as a whole.

When I was twenty-five, I started attending a small Episcopal church in New Haven, Connecticut. Within that community, I also received many gifts: a sense of the responsibility we as Christians have toward the poor and outcast, a deep-seated awareness that God is wholly other and mysterious, and a well-grounded knowledge of the history of the church. But I also retained and became even more attentive to the stories, oracles, psalms, epistles, and visions found in the Bible. In what would outwardly appear to be a very different type of church, the Bible remained for me a constant on my spiritual journey.

I often think about the Bible as being like glasses. I can see without my glasses, but not very well. Things are blurry, without much detail and without much depth. But with my glasses, I can see things clearly that, otherwise, I wouldn't even notice. Even so, Scripture provides us ways of seeing and understanding our lives and our world. By looking at ourselves through the lens of scripture, we can clearly see some things that we otherwise might not even notice: the nature of loving communities that care for the poor and outcast, the presence of a God who is simultaneously intimate and mysterious, and the fact that we are all dependent upon the stories that we tell and the history that has preceded us. For me, this is the power and the wonder of the Bible within our common life together.

CHAPTER ONE

The Book of Judges as Tragedy

I was six years old the first time I was introduced to the book of Judges. Along with about half a dozen other children, I sat at a long, low table, crayon in hand, coloring a picture of a man with incredibly large muscles and incredibly long hair. We sat there, concentrating on our pictures, while the woman at the head of the table read from a Sunday school booklet about the exploits of Samson. We heard how Samson had been blessed by God with super-human strength in order to fight and defeat the evil Philistines. We listened intently to the story of how God had told Samson that the secret to his remarkable strength was found in his long hair, understanding that he must keep his secret and let his hair grow long in order to retain his strength and do all the courageous feats that God had planned for him. So we knew that when the Philistine woman called Delilah came into the story, she was not a good woman. We heard how she boldly cut Samson's hair while he slept and, therefore, robbed him of his power. But we also learned that Samson did not despair, but rather prayed to God for strength one last time and bravely defeated the Philistines by killing many of them in his death. That was how I was introduced to the book of Judges.

If, however, that was my introduction to the book, it was also, in many ways, my conclusion as well. Yes, every three years or so, we would hear the story of Samson again, but that was the only part of the book we ever learned anything about. I never understood why the book was not simply called "The Book of Samson," since he was, I assumed, the only main character in the book! It was not until almost twenty years later that I was introduced to the book for a second time. In my graduate program at Yale, I read Judges as if for the first time and realized not only that it was about a great deal more than Samson, but also that it was a bit more complex than simply the story of a strong man who loses his strength.

I begin this book with my own relationship with Judges because in many ways it parallels the relationship that the church has had with his remarkable book over the centuries. Like me, the church has largely not dealt—or even known—about the book of Judges as a whole, and this, I think, is a real pity. For Judges contains some of the oddest material in all of Scripture. For example, we read stories about military deliverers who often win the war by unusual and certainly unorthodox means. There is the story of Ehud, who secures a victory for Israel by stabbing an enemy king in his own bathroom, and then causes the king's attendants to be late in rounding up their troops; they have to wait until the king is no longer "indisposed." Then we read the story of Deborah who assures the military commander of Israel, Barak, that a victory would be brought about by the hand of a woman; the victory, however, is not won by Deborah herself, but rather by a non-Israelite woman who tricks and murders the enemy general in a most unusual way. After that there is Gideon, who wins a major battle against overwhelming odds by surrounding the enemy by night and breaking pots and lighting torches, which so unnerves the opposing forces that they essentially kill their own troops. Jephthah is so unsure of his ability to lead Israel to victory that he vows that he will sacrifice whatever comes out of his house when he returns victorious from the battle; unfortunately, his own daughter leads the triumphant procession from the house. And, of course, we read the story of Samson, the long-haired strong man who is shorn of both his hair and his strength and eventually kills himself along with a great number of Philistines as his dying act.

The individual characters and the individual stories in Judges are remarkable for their irony, pathos, and occasional humor, yet for the most part they have not been considered as particularly "theological" or "spiritual" when it comes to helping people live their lives.

> *The book of Judges has not been considered as particularly "theological" or "spiritual" when it comes to helping people live their lives.*

That is why when commentators are searching for the "important" portions of narrative in the Old Testament, they more readily turn to Genesis, Exodus, the words of the prophets, and the books of Samuel and Kings to write their works. Even though the organization of the book of Joshua readily lends itself to a multi-week study or sermon series, it is usually passed over in silence.

Overlooking Judges

The two great pillars of the Protestant Reformation, Martin Luther and John Calvin, wrote a great deal about Scripture and produced a vast amount of material commenting on the Bible. Yet, when it came to the book of Judges, neither of these proponents of the Protestant theology of *sola scriptura*—"Scripture alone"—wrote a commentary about it. A great number of theologians and scholars of the eighteenth through the twentieth century, many of them Anglican, attempted to read the Bible with an eye toward its moral lessons and spiritual teachings. But Judges, with its excessive violence and eccentricity, proved a difficult medium to work with.

Thomas Robinson, the rector of St. Mary's Church in Leicester, England, produced an extremely popular volume of sermons that he had preached in his parish during the 1780s. This book, *Scripture Characters*, was pirated and reprinted throughout the first half of the 1800s due to its fame. One of the best known religious books of its time, its sermons focused on biblical characters and were intended "for the serious inquirer after sacred truth." Robinson believed that Scripture's witness to us is largely composed of the wonderful array of characters of upstanding moral fiber, whom we are to imitate: "By looking at the excellencies of others, we are convinced of our own duty, and our sad declensions from it, much more forcibly than by the mere reading of precepts and directions." Scripture, according to Robinson, teaches us how we ought to live by giving us models to follow. Needless to say, when Robinson got around to preaching on the characters of Judges, he completely skipped the entire book and went from a sermon on Joshua, in the preceding book, to one on Eli, in the book of Samuel.

In 1896, Mrs. Annie R. White wrote a whole Bible commentary particularly for the purpose of training teachers of Sunday schools, which were becoming increasingly important both in England and in the United States. Her volume, *Easy Steps for Little Feet: From Genesis to Revelation,* likewise completely leaves out Judges. It would seem as though that book provided too treacherous a path on which "little feet" could take "easy steps." These examples represent literally dozens and dozens of examples of biblical treatises that attempt to read the Bible devotionally or spiritually, but completely pass over Judges.

Judges as Moral Exemplar

When Judges has been dealt with from a practical, spiritual, or theological point of view, the message of the book has usually been exactly what I heard sitting at that long, low table many years ago. Judges is about the stories of people, like Samson, who were "faithful and brave and true," in the words of the hymn, "I Sing a Song of the Saints of God." Their stories relate how these remarkable people serve as examples and models for us to imitate. If Samson was courageous and did not despair in the midst of trouble, then I should remember him when I am feeling afraid or hopeless. This type of "virtue modeling" has long been a standard way of dealing with biblical stories, particularly those of the Old Testament. It is, therefore, no surprise that it was applied to the characters in Judges, even when such an interpretation must completely change the nature of the characters' stories.

The earliest example of this way of dealing with Judges is found in the New Testament itself. In Hebrews 11, the author provides a series of illustrations of the consequences of living faithfully before God. After a general introduction to the subject of faithfulness (11:1–3), the writer concentrates largely upon—in chronological order—Abel, Enoch, Noah (vv. 4–7), Abraham (vv. 8–22), and Moses (vv. 23–28). The passage then turns to the period of the judges, but does not provide any details about them as it did with the previous "heroes of faith." Instead, the writer provides a passing reference to some of the individual judges and winds up explaining not only the purpose of their stories, but the rest of the Old Testament as a whole:

> And what more should I say? For time would fail me to tell of Gideon, Barak, Samson, Jephthah, of David and Samuel and the prophets— who through faith conquered kingdoms, administered justice, obtained promises, shut the mouths of lions, quenched raging fire, escaped the edge of the sword, won strength out of weakness, became mighty in war, put foreign armies to flight (Heb. 11:32–34).

In short, the stories of the judges—according to the writer of Hebrews—tell of the mighty exploits of these Israelite men, who performed all of their remarkable, heroic deeds "through faith." Because they remained faithful to God, they can serve as examples to us to remain faithful. And furthermore, the author of Hebrews goes on to argue, by our following their examples and the example of Christ, we in fact fulfill their stories, we make their stories "perfect" (vv. 39–40).

Understanding the judges as heroes and moral exemplars was common in Christian history even when it strained credulity.

This way of understanding the purpose of Judges is found throughout Christian history. In the early church, seeing the judges as moral exemplars was common, even when it strained credulity. I have already mentioned Jephthah, for example, who sacrifices his own daughter because of a vow that he had made beforehand in the midst of a battle. The leaders of the early church found this story particularly troubling, as indeed it is; the preacher John Chrysostom, however, wrote that the sacrifice of Jephthah's daughter was

> a striking example of providence and clemency; and that it was in care of our race that [God] did not prevent that sacrifice. For if after that vow and promise [God] had forbidden the sacrifice, many also who were subsequent to Jephthah, in the expectation that God would not receive their vows, would have increased the number of such vows, and proceeding on their way would have fallen into child murder. But now, by suffering this vow to be actually fulfilled, [God] put a stop to all such cases in the future."[4]

Chrysostom commends Jephthah for his sacrifice of this daughter because of the far-sightedness of his action, but needless to say, Chrysostom's praise of Jephthah's action is rarely seen as an appropriate perspective on this episode.

Seeing the characters of Judges as providing role-models for our own lives continues even to the present day. In his recent commentary on Judges, Roger Ryan attempts to "give positive readings of the characters of judge-deliverers (chs. 3–16) against the consensus of scholars who generally understand them to be negative role models and anti-heroes."[5] Yet, even with this commendable goal, Ryan often seems to struggle with the material that he has to work with. The characters of the individual judges often seem too chaotic and violent to serve as models for our everyday lives in the twenty-first century. The invitation to "go and do likewise" seems unwise in dealing with Judges.

If it does not tell of the lives of easy, commendable characters whom the reader is to emulate, then what good is the book at all? How can a violent, blood-soaked narrative of morally ambiguous characters be read spiritually, devotionally, or theologically? How, in short, can the book of Judges be read as the Word of God? Does it, to use the words of the Book of Common Prayer, contain anything "necessary to salvation"? I believe that it does, and the goal of this book is to lay out the way in which I see its value for the reader individually and for the whole church generally. But, first, let us understand broadly what the book is about.

The Tragedy of the Book of Judges

Of the two options that I encountered in my own early life with Judges and their parallels in the life of the church with Judges— either by ignoring the book completely or by using it as a straightforward model for faithful living—the former is much easier to do than the second. It is easy to see why Judges has been neither a favorite subject of study in Sunday school rooms nor a compelling topic for sermons. Even a cursory glance through the book reveals that it contains a great deal of violence; in every chapter a war is being waged against some enemy. Even my childhood Sunday school lesson could not evade the fact that Samson was called by God to defeat (and we all knew that was a way of saying "to kill") the Philistines. As the book progresses, in fact, the amount of violence seems to grow from simple statements about skirmishes in the first chapter, all the way to inter-tribal genocide in the final chapter.

The characters in the book, furthermore, when their stories are read apart from our assumptions about the supposed "moral" of these stories, often do not appear heroic at all. In fact they sometimes appear not just fearful, but cowardly. They often are underhanded or dishonest. The violence that they perpetrate against the "enemy" often breaks out against their own friends and families (as with Jephthah), usually with far-reaching results. We may try to read the stories of the judges as examples of "faithfulness," but in order to do so we must also do what the author of Hebrews does and pass over the majority of the book.

How can a violent, blood-soaked narrative of morally ambiguous characters be read spiritually, devotionally, or theologically? Judges is not a book about promise or fulfillment. It is a story of going from "riches to rags" rather than the other way around. It has moments of greatness, no doubt, and scenes of heroism and self-sacrifice. There are also passages that show remarkable humor and a keen sense of irony. But, all in all, the narrative of the book of Judges is a tragedy, rather than a comedy. It stands beside those other great tragedies that we are familiar with in the west: *Oedipus the King, Agamemnon, Romeo and Juliet, Hamlet, Julius Caesar*, and, more recently, the stories found in *Equus, Death of a Salesman*, and *Citizen Kane*. Yet simply because a story does not have a happy ending does not mean it is a bad story, or that its message is unimportant. In fact, tragedies have a great deal to tell us about what it means to be human.

> *How can a violent, blood-soaked narrative of morally ambiguous characters be read spiritually, devotionally, or theologically?*

It seems to me that there are a couple of different ways in which "theological writing" is done in the Bible. One example is the prophetic book of Second Isaiah (chapters 40–55), which makes certain claims about God and wears its theology "on its sleeve." Such a biblical book says that God is compassionate and that, because of that divine compassion, humanity's future is hopeful. The meaning of the book as a whole is tied to such themes; in a sense, Second Isaiah's message is found in what it says directly.

But another way that biblical texts do theology is more oblique. Some portions of Scripture may make very explicit claims, here and there, about who God is and what God does. These texts, however, aren't primarily concerned with proving or defending those claims. They tell stories with beginnings, middles, and ends; through the reading of those stories, the reader is brought to not just a fuller and deeper *knowledge* of God, but an emotional and moving *experience* as well. It seems to me that this is what the gospels do—and also what I think Judges does. If the book is seen as an anthology of separate hero tales, then the order does not matter and the "point" of any particular story can be boiled down and made explicit. But, against the grain of much older historical-critical interpretations, I do not think that's what Judges is about at all. The order and progression and "flow" of the book as a whole is, in a sense, its message.

By dealing with the book of Judges as a tragedy, in its literary and classical sense, I think we can engage with it as a whole and deal with the violence of the book, particularly the final horrific chapters, in a way that is helpful and theologically relevant. For example, if the final chapters of the book are read all on their own, I would be among the first to say that they are not only extremely pessimistic about Israel's future, but theologically empty and worthless as well. But when seen as the last, pitiful gasp of the downfall of the character of Israel—after a series of truly tragic downward turns—then their cautionary (and theological) meaning comes to the fore. I also believe that reading the book of Judges as a tragedy enables us, as contemporary readers, to make sense of the book as a whole, which is how we usually read things of this nature anyway.

Because tragedies function to warn us of the dramatic consequences of the flaws to which we are all liable, we often would rather either ignore their warnings or try to rationalize and gloss over them. Human beings generally do not like thinking of themselves as weak or frail, and this is, perhaps, our greatest weakness and flaw. In order to hear the testimony that tragedies provide for us and to appreciate what they have to tell us,

> *Reading the book of Judges as a tragedy enables us, as contemporary readers, to make sense of the book as a whole.*

we must be very intentional about listening to them. What, then, is tragedy about and how ought we hear what it tells us? Historically, all treatments of the nature of tragedy are based on the first major historical treatment of it, that of Aristotle.

In his book *Poetics*, Aristotle provides a definition of "tragedy" that serves as the basis for practically every discussion of this art form down to the present day:

> A tragedy, then, is the imitation of an action that is serious and also, as having magnitude, complete in itself; in language with pleasurable accessories, each kind brought in separately in the parts of the work; in a dramatic, not in a narrative form; with incidents arousing pity and fear, wherewith to accomplish its catharsis of such emotions."[6]

Aristotle understood tragedy to be a type of theatrical performance, and probably had in mind *Oedipus the King* as a primary example of this type of art. Tragedy, for him, was about important, serious events; it was written in pleasing, artful language; and it had the goal of bringing forth "pity and fear" in the audience, so that these strong emotions could be better dealt with (cleansed, thus bringing catharsis) by the audience. The definition seems to imply that the emotions of pity and fear are strong and can, like an illness, cause harm to those who have them in excess. Tragedy provides a means by which we can keep our over-sensitivity (pity) or our unwillingness to be involved (fear) in check. By watching the downfall of an important character, either because of his or her moral failures or because of simple human fallibility, the audience can exercise these emotions and can deal with them more appropriately in their everyday lives.

The literary critic Ruby Cohn highlights the way in which tragedy is an almost universal art form. She notes that almost every culture has certain writings at whose heart lies a paradox, for tragedy produces two opposite effects in those who experience it.[7] It is a form of art based on human suffering that also produces pleasure in the audience. For many modern literary critics, tragedy is not only about the "cleansing" of pity and fear. Tragedy is also about the deriving of some sort of pleasure, although the pleasure that tragedy gives us is not a masochistic glee over the suffering itself. When Charles Foster Kane dies with the word "Rosebud" on his lips at the beginning and at the ending of *Citizen Kane*, we do not feel joy at the downfall of this great, tragic character. The pleasure that the movie brings forth is something deeper than simple entertainment.

I suspect that we find joy in watching that movie or *Romeo and Juliet* because it gives us a way of dealing not only with our own pity and fear, but with the chaos that is a part of our lives. We live in a chaotic world, a world just as susceptible to violence and injustice as when the book of Judges was composed. Tragedy provides us a way of grappling with our world by neither allowing us to feel morally superior to its tragic characters, nor by leaving us awash in a sea of relativism and pointlessness. Tragedy's pleasure comes from an understanding of one's own human nature and having the will and, through the tragedy, the motivation to deal with some of one's own weaknesses and errors.

I do not wish to argue that Judges was written as a "tragedy" in the Greek sense. It is, after all, not a play, but a series of small stories. To use Aristotle's words, Judges unfolds in "narrative" and not "dramatic" form. Also, I do not think that the editors of the book had Aristotle in the back of their minds as they compiled and edited the final form of the book. I do think, however, that having "tragedy" as one lens through which we can read the book is an extremely helpful way of understanding what is going on and for getting a grasp on why the book reads the way it does. It is also, I believe, a key that can help us see what the book has to say to us theologically and spiritually.

If tragedy has to do with the downfall of a central, important character, then who is the central character of Judges? Most commentators answer the question by pointing to the title of the book: the central characters of the book are the "judges" themselves. I think, however, that this misses the overall message of the book, its overarching plot, and the theological experience of the book as a whole. We miss the point of the book as a whole if we see each of the individual judges as the main characters of the book.

The central character of the book is Israel itself. From the first verse ("After the death of Joshua, the Israelites inquired of the LORD, 'Who shall go up first for us against the Canaanites, to fight against them?'") to the final verse of the book ("In those days there was no king in Israel; all the people did what was right in their own eyes"),

Israel as a whole is the single unifying character that the book is about. Yes, of course, the exploits of the judges provide the driving force of the many different plots and scenes that are gathered together within the book. And yes, the wars and maneuverings of the oppressive kings provide the complication that spurs the plot ahead. But looked at as a whole, theologically coherent tragedy, the central character is Israel itself.

It is Israel that sets out for victory at the beginning and it is Israel that falls into violence, chaos, and anarchy at the end. Throughout the book, we trace the steps that Israel takes down the long spiral that leads to its near-destruction. It is Israel itself that sins, that falls into oppression, that cries out to God, that is rescued by the deliverer-judge, and that falls into sin once more after the death of the deliverer. As we move, step by step, through the plot of the tragedy, we see Israel either in the hands of individual strongmen or acting on its own authority, always falling into apostasy. And, as it maneuvers this way and that, Israel's downfall becomes ever more sure. But, from beginning to end, the story focuses only on Israel as its central character. This is a tale of the tragedy of Israel.

For this reason, the book of Judges is a vitally important witness in the scriptures. Its witness is not one that we can ignore, because it is a cautionary tale that warns us to pay attention to those aspects of our religious and moral life that are particularly dangerous precisely because they are so important. And, by patiently hearing its witness in all of its fullness, we may also recognize the hope that it can bring us.

The Assembling of the Book of Judges

Judges is one of the most clearly organized books in Hebrew scripture. Practically any commentary on the book will, more or less, have the same identical outline of the book, which is truly saying something in light of the often contentious and critical nature of biblical scholarship! Part of the reason for the clarity of the parts of the book is probably tied to the history of how it was composed in stages, various blocks being added piece by piece until, long after the events it depicts, the book reached the form in which we have it today.

The history of the composition or assembling of the book of Judges probably occurred in a four-step process. All of the steps of this process are clearly visible in the final form of the book as it stands in our Bibles today. Sometimes, the various stages in the composition cause the final form to look slightly disjointed, but if a reader understands how the book was put together over time, these disjunctions will contribute to an appreciation of the book instead of detracting from it. The four phases that the book went through to reach its final form are these:

- First, relatively small stories about different military heroes were orally told and passed down independently within the separate tribes where each had lived.
- Second, these separate stories were collected together to form a longer series of "deliverer stories."
- Third, an introduction was added to the beginning of the series and the individual tales themselves were each standardized to follow a similar storyline.
- Fourth, the collection was incorporated into a larger story that outlined the period from Israel's coming into the land of Canaan (in Joshua) to the destruction of Jerusalem and the Exile (in Second Kings). This incorporation of the collection involved adding another introduction onto the beginning of the book and the attaching of two additional stories onto the end.

This four-phrase process produced the book of Judges as it exists today. I'd like to go through the process and describe how each of the stages affected and reworked the material that it had at hand.

The stories of the judges probably began exactly like that—as stories that were orally told about the individual leaders. A clue to the "oral background" of much of the material in the book is found in what is called the episodic nature of its stories. Today we are most familiar with the idea of an "episode" when thinking about television programs like "Law and Order," which occur in weekly, serial installments that are connected by the show's characters, such as Assistant D. A. Jack McCoy or Detective Olivia

A clue to the "oral background" of much of the material in the book is found in the episodic nature of its stories.

Benson. Each week, their shows begin at basically the same point. Then, usually within the first few minutes, a complication is thrown into the plot. Then the characters attempt to deal with the problem by solving the crime or judging the case, which often causes further complications. This continues until, near the end of the program, the problem is resolved and the characters return to the state in which they began the program. Whether the show is a "situation comedy" or a "medical drama" or a "crime-scene investigation" program, the way in which the show's plot runs is very similar.

With television programs like "Law and Order," whose run extended into many years, there may be some minor character development, or some character changes. But generally, each episode is complete in and of itself. The world at the end of the show is basically the same as the world at the beginning of the show. This is particularly helpful for television programs that go into syndication.

For example, when I was much younger, I would come home from school every day and watch an episode of "Gilligan's Island," a comedy show about seven zany individuals who were stranded on a deserted island. Although originally it was broadcast once a week, by the time I encountered the show it had already gone into syndication and was broadcast every day at 3:30, just in time for junior high children to watch it (which was just the level of humor that "Gilligan's Island" dealt in). It did not matter whether the episode was one of the early ones shot in black and white, or one of the later ones shot in color; the characters were always the same and the plot always had to do with the seven castaways almost (but not quite) finding a way off the island. When the episodes are rebroadcast, it is not absolutely necessary that they be shown in the exact order that they were originally broadcast. Since there is so little character development or overall plot change, each episode can be watched and understood with little or no reference to any other episodes.

In a very similar way, people tell stories. Whether they be jokes, or fables, or historical vignettes, or a recounting of what happened on the way home from work, stories are usually told in such a way that they can be understood with little explicit reference outside themselves. This is the nature of "episodic storytelling." The stories of the men and women in the central part of the book of Judges are like

this, and this characteristic points to the probability that these stories were originally oral. Whether read or heard aloud, each of the
judge stories can be appreciated and understood in and of itself.
Each of the stories begins at a certain point; then a complication is
brought into the plot, which causes (usually) further complications,
which eventually boils up to a climax, after which things return to
the point at which they began.

The setting of these stories occurs in a time when Israel was not a
kingdom but a loose tribal confederacy ruled by "judges," some of
whom were military leaders, some warriors acting on their own, and
some—like the prophetess Deborah—on a reli-
gious mission. Furthermore, because of the importance of place names in the various stories and the
tribal background of many of the tales, it very well
may be that each of the stories was told in different
places about local heroes. Thus, the story of Ehud
(3:12–30) might have been specifically told in the
land of Benjamin, a southern tribe, because Ehud comes from Benjamin and the enemy comes from Moab, a southern country near
Benjamin. On the other hand, the story of Deborah and Barak (4:1–
24) might have been told by northern tribes, since Deborah the judge
comes from Ephraim in the north, her general Barak from Naphtali,
and the king they defeat rules from the city of Hazor, a city in the far
north of Israel. The stories, therefore, arose and were told in local
circles and were probably originally focused on past dangers and
exploits of the tribe itself.

One final word about the oral, episodic nature of the stories as
they originally were told is in order. When heard with no regard to
their relative placement in the wider book, the stories can be seen as
tales glorifying the exploits of famous tribal leaders in the past. It is
probable that each of the stories of the judges was originally told in
order to hold up the central military leader as a hero, as one who,
through the skill and might granted by God, was able to fight and
defend the survival of the tribe. These stories were originally told to
highlight the virtues of their central characters. As we read them
today, however, we do not have the tales of the judges as individual
stories because at some point they were collected and developed by

> The setting of these stories occurs in a time when Israel was not a kingdom but a loose tribal confederacy ruled by "judges," some of whom were military leaders.

editors into a longer story, while simultaneously retaining their original episodic nature.

At some point in time, these individual stories were written down and collected together into an anthology or a series. This collection of the central block of stories involved three characteristics that we can still see in our own final form of the book. First, when the stories were collected, the question would have naturally arisen: in what order are the stories to be placed? Since each of the stories is complete in itself, they could have, theoretically, been placed in any order whatsoever. One of the principles of the ordering of the stories might have been that they run, generally, from short (in the first half of the book) to long (in the second half). Thus, in the first half of the book, the story of Ehud is approximately eighteen verses long (3:12–20) and the story of Deborah is twenty-four (4:1–24), with a poetic appendix in chapter 5. Compare this to the second half of the book, where the story of Gideon is ninety-seven verses long (6:1–8:32); the story of Jephthah fifty-seven (10:6–12:7); and the story of Samson is ninety-six (13:1–16:31). This basic consideration of length may have caused the compilers to generally order the stories in this particular way.

A second characteristic that was introduced when the oral stories were written and compiled into a collection was the introduction of the "minor judges" into the book. These characters were leaders who had few or no stories about them and their heroism. Scattered in the midst of the collection, these individuals appear alongside the other major judges: Shamgar (3:31), Tola (10:1–2), Jair (10:3–5), Ibzan (12:8–10), Elon (12:11–12), and Abdon (12:13–15).

A final characteristic of this collection of stories is its national rather than tribal character.

When they were combined with each other, the stories were no longer about tribal heroes who lead skirmishes for their small clan, but rather about how these heroes fought on behalf of Israel as a whole. It is Israel as a whole that is oppressed; it is all Israel that cries out to God for help and fights under the leadership of the judge, and Israel as a whole that is delivered. One can see how, when all the stories were combined, what were originally individual tales took on a wider and broader perspective. What was once a tribal story becomes Israel's story. At this point in the development of the book, the central "character" also becomes Israel—the earlier focus on the individual heroes shifts to the overall experience of Israel as a whole. In other words, Israel becomes the point of the book.

The next step in the development of Judges involved adding an introduction to the beginning and the regularizing of the basic plot lines of many of the stories. This introduction to the book (2:6–3:11) makes its opening verses conform to the ending of the book of Joshua:

> After these things Joshua son of Nun, the servant of the Lord, died, being one hundred and ten years old. They buried him in his own inheritance at Timnath-serah, which is in the hill country of Ephraim, north of Mount Gaash.

> Israel served the Lord all the days of Joshua, and all the days of the elders who outlived Joshua and had known all the work that the Lord did for Israel (Joshua 24:29–31).

> The people worshipped the Lord all the days of Joshua, and all the days of the elders who outlived Joshua, who had seen all the great work that the Lord had done for Israel. Joshua son of Nun, the servant of the Lord, died at the age of one hundred and ten years. So they buried him within the bounds of his inheritance in Timnath-heres, in the hill country of Ephraim, north of Mount Gaash. Moreover, that whole generation was gathered to their ancestors, and another generation grew up after them, who did not know the Lord or the work that he had done for Israel (Judges 2:7–10).

After this formula is repeated, the introduction continues by laying out the primary narrative turning points that the editors will also incorporate into many of the stories. Israel sins, which causes God to oppress Israel through the attacks of foreign enemies. God then raises up a judge-deliverer to defeat the foreign enemy, which leads to Israel falling back into sin after the death of the judge.

Once the introduction establishes the major turning points of the stories, the reader is prepared to see these turning points throughout each of the following stories. What is interesting, however, about these turning points is that they slowly disappear as the different stories are told. In each of the successive stories, the turning points are first explicitly quoted, then are occasionally alluded to, then occasionally drop out. This incremental loss of the order established by the introduction has the effect of paralleling the loss of the order of the society of Israel as a whole. What was once a series of stories told episodically in a formal cycle is now a long narrative, in which the storylines become more and more random. This slow loss of the regular outline of the stories is one of the primary things that we will notice as we go through the book. The overall decline of the order is directly tied to the tragic vision of the book as a whole and provides an important key for understanding the message and witness of what the book is primarily about.

Finally, the introduction and story collection was incorporated into a larger block of material in the Bible called the "Deuteronomistic History." In 1957 a German scholar named Martin Noth suggested that the original writings in the book of Judges, along with other earlier traditional materials in the Hebrew Bible, were used by the individual or group of individuals who compiled and edited a grand history of Israel. This history, which scholars have named the "Deuteronomistic History," or simply "the History," tells the story of Israel's entry and conquering of the land of Canaan (Joshua), through the period of the judges (Judges) and the establishment of the monarchy under Saul and David (1 and 2 Samuel), to the division of the kingdom of David into the northern kingdom of Israel and the southern kingdom of Judah (1 Kings), to the eventual destruction of first Samaria in the north and then Jerusalem in the south (2 Kings). In this way it traces the story of Israel from a relatively successful state through to its eventual dissolution and destruction. The History is, therefore, a very large tragedy, whose primary message is how continual rebellion against God and sin leads to a loss of freedom and eventual death.

The original writings in the book of Judges, along with others in the Hebrew Bible, were used by those who compiled and edited a grand history of Israel.

It is, for that reason, no surprise that the smaller story of the book of Judges was incorporated so easily into the larger History, since their purposes are very similar. The final editor had only to provide two pieces of material to make the inclusion complete and smooth.

First, still another introduction was placed ahead of the original introduction: "After the death of Joshua, the Israelites inquired of the LORD, 'Who shall go up first for us against the Canaanites, to fight against them?'" (1:1). This "prequel" introduction picks up from the conclusion of the book of Joshua, in which Joshua and the whole generation of those who entered the land of Canaan die and are buried. This new introduction provides a snapshot of the tragic plotline that will unfold both in the book of Judges, as well as in the Deuteronomistic History as a whole. Israel goes from a state of relative success and happiness, through a series of failures, until finally God withdraws blessing from Israel and they are no longer assured of protection or success.

Second, the Deuteronomistic editor added two longer stories onto the *end* of the judge series to serve as concluding stories—Micah and the conquest of Dan, and the war against Gibeah. These final sections have many parallels with the newer introduction. By adding these conclusions, the editor was able to highlight both the radical difference between how the book begins and how it ends (thus making explicit the tragic nature of the whole), as well as to provide a transition to the following book of Samuel.

The Title of "Judges"

Before I bring this first chapter to a close, I want to discuss briefly the traditional title of the book. The name of the book, "Judges," conjures up in our English minds images of courtrooms, pounding gavels, and black robes. The name, however, comes from the relatively few times that the title is given to one or another of these deliverers: Othniel (3:10), Deborah (4:4–5), Tola (10:2), Jair (10:3), Jephthah (12:7), Ibzan (12:8–9), Elon (12:11), Abdon (12:13–14), and Samson (15:20). One can see that the majority of the places that "judges" appear in the book are in chapters 10 through 12, with Othniel, Deborah, and Samson thrown in for good measure. So why is the book called "Judges"? What does "judging" mean in the context of these stories?

Jo Ann Hackett has noted that the Hebrew verb *shafat*, "to judge," is—as in English—often tied to "decision-making contexts" in the Old Testament. The judge in ancient Israel was "not only responsible for the administration of justice but could also perform duties that include some sort of governing."[8] It is interesting, therefore, to look back at the list of "judges" in the book and note that only in the case of Othniel, the first "judge," is the deliverance of Israel from the power of the oppressing king tied to his "judging": "The spirit of the LORD came upon [Othniel], and he judged Israel; he went out to war, and the LORD gave King Cushan-rishathaim of Aram into his hand; and his hand prevailed over Cushan-rishathaim" (3:10). In all other cases, the judgeship of the deliverer is associated either with activities before the military campaign (as with Deborah) or afterwards, in the aftermath of the war. While these may be stories of "judges," we get very few stories about that aspect of their role. The stories mostly highlight their roles as military leaders, as "deliverers."

This confusion of roles—a charismatic military leader who, after the battle, is expected to take on the role of "judge"—might be a clue to one of the underlying messages of the book. What qualities are needed to execute a strategic military victory? Strength? Quick decisiveness? Impulsiveness? Are these the same qualities for a long career in adjudicating disputes and meting out justice? Perhaps; perhaps not. What are the qualities that make a good leader? What are the qualities that make a bad leader? The book of Judges may provide us a way of thinking seriously about these types of issues.

> *What are the qualities that make a good or bad leader? The book of Judges provides us with a way of thinking seriously about these questions.*

The term "judges" also raises up another theme that one like "deliverers" would not raise. As in English, the Hebrew noun "a judge" (*shofet*) is associated with the word "justice" (*mishpat*) and the verb "to judge" (*shafat*). The three words are all interconnected: a "judge" "judges" according to systems of "justice." Throughout the book of Judges, one of the themes that we will return to in one way or another again and again will be this: What does "justice" actually mean? What is the "just" or "right" thing for God to do when Israel sins and turns its back on both God and the covenant agreement that they have? What is the "just" or "right" thing for God to do when Israel cries out under the oppression they suffer? And finally, what is the "just" or "right" thing for God to do when Israel repeatedly sins or when Israel repeatedly suffers under oppression? Is "justice" a simple formula, or does it change as circumstances change?

Judges may not be the happiest book in the Bible, but it is certainly one of the most artful and beautifully written. Not only that, I believe its message is one of the most important for those who are dealing with community, particularly broken community, and are seeking a way of thinking about what it means to live in community more fully. Judges is occasionally humorous, often shocking, usually ironic, but it is always important.

Back When Life Was Simple: The Introductions

In my classes on the interpretation of the Old Testament, I try to help students read unfamiliar stories with a sympathetic eye and, what is even more difficult, familiar stories with a fresh eye. It is one thing to read a story one has never read before as if for the first time and try to understand what it is about. It is, in fact, simplicity itself! But it is extremely difficult to read a story or a poem that we feel we know like the back of our hand in such a way that we can see something new or unexpected or truly meaningful in it. Human beings have a tendency to confuse "familiarity" with "understanding." When we are familiar with something—whether a story, or a place, or a person—we are very quick to believe that we "know" it, that we "understand" it. This often makes reading well-known classics extremely boring.

When, furthermore, the text we are familiar with is the Bible, this confusion of familiarity with understanding is not only the seedbed for boredom, but can also produce self-defeating attitudes, such as pride, anger, or complacency. It is an interesting fact that when someone tells me that they "read and study the Bible a lot," I have absolutely no idea what sort of person they are. The texts that we, as Christians, claim to be the "Word of God," those stories and poems and letters that have been "written for our instruction," ancient texts that we claim "contain all things necessary to salvation," can produce readers who are kind, patient, humble, curious, and loving. But they can also produce readers who are judgmental, intolerant, arrogant, closed-minded, and hurtful. What is the difference? I think at least some of the basis for the difference lies in whether people come to the Bible with an attitude of wanting to hear a "living word" or whether they come wanting to hear what they already think they know about what the Bible says.

In the class, as we work our way through the texts of the Old Testament over the course of nine months, I have several tricks that I invite the students to use in order to "defamiliarize" the stories and poems that we read, in order to hear the texts differently or more deeply. I call these tricks (appropriately enough) Heller's Rules of Reading. The first rule, which I mention as we begin reading the first chapter of Genesis, is this:

> Whenever you begin to read a story or a poem, always pay special attention to the very first thing the author or narrator or poet writes. Always pay attention to the very first words, the first verses, the first few lines (for poems) or the first paragraph (for stories).

Often in reading stories, we believe the real "punch" of the plot is wrapped up, almost solely, in the climax, where the action reaches its culmination and from which the story reaches its resolution. While I acknowledge, of course, the importance of climaxes for stories, I emphasize to the students the importance of where the story begins, and how the author or narrator initiates the plot and starts the ball rolling. Authors often spend a great deal of time wrestling with the very first line of a short story or a novel. Why? Because how a story begins is almost as important as how a story ends.

Then I point out to the students the opening of Charles Dickens' *A Tale of Two Cities* and how in itself it sets up all the conflicts found not only throughout the novel but also, historically, in the time period in which the novel is set:

> It was the best of times, it was the worst of times, it was the age of wisdom, it was the age of foolishness, it was the epoch of belief, it was the

epoch of incredulity, it was the season of Light, it was the season of Darkness, it was the spring of hope, it was the winter of despair, we had everything before us, we had nothing before us, we were all going direct to Heaven, we were all going direct the other way—in short, the period was so.

That long opening sentence is the perfect base upon which Dickens could write about such an ambiguous and divisive time as late eighteenth-century Europe. The first sentence is, in a way, the most important of the whole book.

This is true of almost every great narrative work. One can often get a fresh perspective on what a book means by simply looking at the first line:

"Who's there?" (Shakespeare's *Hamlet*)

"Half way along the road we have to go,
I found myself obscured in a great forest,
Bewildered, and I knew I had lost the way." (Dante's *Inferno*)

"It was a bright cold day in April, and the clocks were striking thirteen." (Orwell's *1984*)

"It is a pleasure to burn." (Bradbury's *Fahrenheit 451*)

By paying attention to how a story begins, as readers we can better see how the story unfolds and, therefore, may get a better or deeper grasp on what the text as a whole might mean.

This is, of course, no less true of biblical texts. The beginnings of biblical books very often (if not always) provide the base upon which the structure of the rest of the plot is built. And, by paying attention to those beginnings, we can often get hints at ways of understanding the "rest of the story."

> *The beginning of any book of the Bible usually gives us important clues as to how we should understand and interpret the whole story.*

What Is Behind the Two Introductions?

As I mentioned in the first chapter, the book of Judges is a highly structured narrative. It is clear that, however the traditions and stories originated, when brought together into this continuous story, they were carefully chosen and placed next to one another to form the book as a whole. That is why Heller's First Rule of

Reading is important when dealing with Judges. We need to notice the way this book begins because it begins not with one introduction but with two.

The question "Why are there two different introductions?" can be answered in two very different ways. The question can be seen as a "diachronic" or a "synchronic" issue. A "diachronic" question about a book or collection of texts is one that tries to understand the way a book is organized by looking at how a text came to be "through" (*dia* in Greek) a span of "time" (*chronos*). If, for example, we ask, "Why does the Bible have an Old Testament and a New Testament?" a diachronic answer would discuss the formation and collection of the Old Testament books at the end of the first millennium BCE and early decades of the first millennium CE, the life and death of Jesus of Nazareth, and the later formation and collection of the New Testament books that dealt with Jesus, which occurred in the first few centuries of the Common Era. In other words, the answer relies on the progression of time to explain the question.

A "synchronic" question about a book or collection is one that tries to understand the way a book is organized by looking at the way it looks in its final form (*syn*, "together" in Greek, and *chronos*, "time"). So the question, "Why does the Bible have an Old Testament and a New Testament?" seen from a synchronic perspective, might be answered by noting how certain basic religious images or ideas are treated similarly and differently in the two collections, and that this "similar yet different" way of understanding God or humanity or creation is at the heart of the way that Christians think and live out their faith. Such an answer doesn't necessarily have to rely on chronological timelines to answer the question. It can deal with the final form of the Bible quite apart from speculating about how the Bible came to be.

An example of this from modern media is the various movies that make up the *Star Wars* double trilogy. The movies were created from 1977 to 2005 and consist of six separate movies that fall roughly into two groups of three. An interesting aspect of the *Star Wars* series is that the earliest movie, originally simply called *Star Wars*, was eventually the fourth movie and was renamed *A New Hope*. If you wanted to discuss the storyline of the entire series, you could do so in two different ways. You could trace the history of the series through time and discuss the move-making techniques of George Lucas, the director, beginning in 1977 with the original movie, through the final two movies of the series, then through the first three movies of the "prequel." This would be looking at the Star Wars series diachronically. But you could also treat the series as it appears as a final product and trace the basic plot outline, beginning with *Episode I: The Phantom Menace* (released in 1999), through the next two episodes, then picking up the storyline with *Episode IV: A New Hope* (released in 1977), and concluding with the sixth and final episode released in 1983. This would be looking at the Star Wars series synchronically.

Both ways of understanding texts—even modern "texts" like movies—are important. Both ways of thinking about texts are helpful in understanding why books look the way they do and, therefore, the way they mean what they mean.

A diachronic way of answering the question, "Why are there two prologues to the book of Judges?" was answered near the end of the previous chapter. Many scholars think that the two introductions were added at two different times for two different purposes. The first introduction was perhaps added when the book of Judges became a part of the larger Deuteronomistic History. It even may have been one of the last things included in the book. In its general sweep it goes from a time of relative success in taking the land to a time of dismal failure, much like the general sweep of the whole Deuteronomistic History itself. The second introduction was perhaps the original introduction to the collection of stories about the deliverers and judges. It also seems to be "Deuteronomistic," with themes that are present in the larger history, such as the effects of sin and its punishment, but is clearly not a simple continuation of the first introduction. This, then, is an answer to the question, "Why are there two introductions to the Book of Judges?" from a diachronic perspective: they come from two different times.

> In its general sweep the first introduction to Judges describes Israel's trajectory from a time of relative success and tribal harmony to a time of dismal failure and violence.

A synchronic way of answering the question will approach it very differently. It might look at the similarities and the differences between the two introductions. For example, both prologues begin with a reference to Joshua:

"After the death of Joshua, the Israelites inquired of the LORD ..." (1:1).

"When Joshua dismissed the people, the Israelites all went to their own inheritances ..." (2:6).

Both references use the figure of Joshua as a turning point, as a way of introducing something new. Furthermore, the juxtaposition of Joshua's death and then his dismissal of the people assures that the reader cannot miss the fact that two very different blocks of material have been set here at the beginning of the book. If the two introductions were reversed, with the consequences of Joshua's dismissal of the people coming first, followed by the consequences of Joshua's death, the oddness of the story would be harder to grasp. But now, with Joshua's death mentioned *before* his dismissal of the people, a perceptive reader will suspect that something strange is going on. As a result, the two disparate references to Joshua assure that the two blocks retain their integrity while simultaneously sitting at the beginning of the stories of the judges.

The two introductions also have similar endings. After recounting the dismal failures on the part of Israel throughout, both end with God's withdrawal of the promise to protect Israel and give it the land of Canaan. At the end of the first prologue, the angel of the LORD appears and witnesses that God had made a promise to uphold the covenant forever if only Israel would in turn remain true and refrain from worshipping the gods of the Canaanites. Israel, however, had not upheld its part of the covenant and, therefore, God would not drive out the Canaanites; they would coexist with the Israelites and compete for land, water, and food. Likewise, at the end of the second introduction, God makes a very similar speech, in which he notes that he will no longer remove the Canaanites because of the disobedience of Israel: "I will no longer drive out before them any of the nations that Joshua left when he died" (2:21). The prologue ends by noting the groups that were left, which intermarry with Israel and whose gods are worshipped by Israel:

Because Israel was unfaithful to the covenant, God's protection and the gift of the land of Canaan was withdrawn.

So the Israelites lived among the Canaanites, the Hittites, the Amorites, the Perizzites, the Hivites, and the Jebusites; and they took their daughters as wives for themselves, and their own daughters they gave to their sons; and they worshiped their gods (3:5–6).

The two introductions, however, also have important and distinctive differences. The first provides a preview of the book of Judges by tracing out how Israel goes from relative success and cooperation, through increasing failures until finally, in the "character" of the tribe of Dan, being repulsed by the Amorites and unable to live where they wished. Along the way, six tiny stories are inserted, each of which provides glimpses of themes we will find later in the judge stories. The final story recounts the reversal of God's promise of the land. Thus the flow of the narrative in the first introduction can be thought of as a descending line, going down from success to failure.

The second introduction also provides a glimpse of the rest of the book—not in a linear way, but in an episodic and cyclical way. After a short paragraph setting the time of the book as occurring "after the death of Joshua," the bulk of this second prologue lists the various "movements" that are supposed to occur, explicitly or implicitly, in each of the following stories of the judges. Each of the major deliverance stories in the first part of Judges follows a pattern: they begin with the Israelites sinning, which incites God to hand them over to their enemies, at which point God raises up a judge to deliver them from the enemy. When, however, the judge dies (at the end of each particular cycle), Israel falls back into sin and behaves "worse than their ancestors," which starts the cycle all over again. The introduction ends with God refusing to drive out "any of the nations Joshua left when he died," and the results of that refusal. The flow of this second introduction can thus be thought of as a cycle, tracing the repeating scenes in the various stories that will follow.

As each judge dies, Israel falls back into sin and treachery, which starts the whole cycle over again.

Before we turn our attention to the two prologues in detail, notice how this combination of the two together provides the perfect beginning to the book as a whole. When the "descending line" of the first introduction is combined with the "cycle" of the second introduction, the result is a downward spiral, a "cycle" in which each successive story descends further down the slope toward chaos. And this is, precisely, what we will find in the stories and, in a wider sense, in the book as a whole.

Furthermore—and this is an extremely important point—the descending spiral from order to chaos is primarily accomplished in the stories by dismantling the pattern so carefully constructed in the second introduction. Each of the elements (sin, oppression, deliverance, death of the judge) is clearly and obviously present in the opening story of Othniel:

> The Israelites did what was evil in the sight of the Lord, forgetting the Lord their God, and worshiping the Baals and the Asherahs.
>
> Therefore the anger of the Lord was kindled against Israel, and he sold them into the hand of King Cushan-rishathaim of Aram-naharaim; and the Israelites served Cushan-rishathaim eight years.
>
> But when the Israelites cried out to the Lord, the Lord raised up a deliverer for the Israelites, who delivered them, Othniel son of Kenaz, Caleb's younger brother. The spirit of the Lord came upon him, and he judged Israel; he went out to war, and the Lord gave King Cushan-rishathaim of Aram into his hand; and his hand prevailed over Cushan-rishathaim. So the land had rest forty years.
>
> Then Othniel son of Kenaz died.
>
> The Israelites again did what was evil in the sight of the Lord (3:7–12).

However, every story following Othniel will either not explicitly mention one of these elements or will leave one or two out, will reverse them, or will otherwise mix them up. The result is that each successive story is less clearly organized according to the pattern that has been established in the second introduction.

The importance of this for understanding what Judges as a whole is about cannot be overstated. Unlike some biblical books whose central message is found in a few important passages, which are surrounded with other types of supporting material, the message of Judges is found precisely within the plot itself. If an interpreter takes any particular story out of the overall plot and tries to discuss the meaning (theological, ethical, or any other type) of the episode apart from the overall purpose and meaning of the book as a whole, the effect would be distorted. Every story is important; every scene is vital. Each of them is like a pearl that is placed on a string that eventually forms a beautiful necklace. But taking a look at a few of the more interesting pearls does not give us an impression, or an appreciation, of the necklace as a whole. And, in the case of Judges, the whole necklace, the whole plot, the whole book is where its meaning lies. We will arrive at the conclusion, in which the pattern has completely disappeared, wondering where Israel has gone so very wrong. By that point, however, we realize that the tragedy of Israel and its judges, summed up in the conclusion and essentially found throughout the plot as a whole, was already hinted at in the very first two chapters of the book.

> *Unlike some biblical books, whose central message is found in a few important passages, the message of Judges is found within the plot itself.*

The First Introduction (1:1–2:5)

The first prologue to the book of Judges alternates between six tiny stories, or vignettes, and four accounts of military successes or failures. This alternating, flip-flop quality of the first introduction prepares us for reading the book as a whole. Like a good teacher, it provides us with very short stories which for the most part are easily grasped and understood. These little vignettes also contain themes that we will see throughout the book as a whole, themes such as cooperation and betrayal, divine retribution and human complicity, surprising initiative and heartbreaking loss.

Sandwiched between these stories are short reports of military activity. These brief "bulletins" also introduce us to a major motif of the book of Judges: war. The stories depicted are not to be read and understood simply on their own, but against the backdrop of warfare. Both stories and reports work together to provide us with a way of understanding both. The first three stories, with their interspersed military reports, are hopeful, showing a victorious Israel in an optimistic light, while the military reports only give positive accounts of Israel's victories with no mention of any (Israelite) loss of life.

The second set of three stories in the introduction, along with their interspersed military reports, are less hopeful and show the Israelites as betraying, underhanded, and eventually faithless in their relationship with their God. As one might suspect, the military

reports likewise are more pessimistic and introduce military stalemates and defeats for Israel. Overall, the six stories (and four military reports) of the first introduction to the book take the reader
from a time of success to a time of failure, from a time of cooperation to a time of simple self-preservation, from a time of harmony
with God to a time of betrayal of God.

Let us take a look at each of these sections, see how the stories
work together, and get a grasp on how this first introduction to the
book might prepare us for what comes later.

If I were to outline the first few stories of the book of Judges, I
might title them "a happy beginning," and together they look something this:[9]

- Story: Judah, Simeon, and tribal cooperation
- Report: Military success
- Story: Adoni-bezek and divine retribution
- Report: Military success
- Story: Achsah and feminine initiative

Notice the flip-flop quality I mentioned before. The three stories
and the two military reports alternate in such a way that the whole
complex—all five parts—work together to produce a "whole" passage, or a triple-decker literary sandwich.

Let us, therefore, take a look at this happy beginning.

The very first verse of the book of Judges is remarkable, particularly when we are aware of the contents of the rest of the book. Here,
we are told, the victorious leader Joshua has died and Israel's first
response is to turn to God for direction. Throughout the first part of
the book, when the death of a leader occurs, Israel will relapse, or
wander, or fall into sinful and harmful ways of acting. Here, at the
beginning, things are much better. Instead of turning away or else
turning to another leader to guide them, Israel itself—as a whole—
takes up the fullness of its relationship with God and seeks direction
on what they should do next. And the direction comes: "Judah shall
go up. I hereby give the land into his hand" (1:2).

Judah's response is similarly unusual in light of much of the latter
part of the book. The tribe of Judah asks its partner tribe, Simeon,
for help in its exploits, and promises to help Simeon later. Simeon,

furthermore, agrees to cooperate wholeheartedly. Eventually Judges will end with tribes and individual Israelites all doing "what was right in their own eyes" (21:25), with the implication that what they are doing is not right objectively, or rationally, or in the sight of God. By the end of the book, Israel will be a fractured, violated society, rife with civil war. But here, in the beginning, Israel not only inquires of God as a unified people, but also the tribes of Judah and Simeon fulfill God's command in a unified front. Judah, moreover, will fulfill his promise to help Simeon later in the chapter. The story is brief and sweet.

The account of Israel's first military expedition in Judges is also unusual in light of the rest of the book. God's command to Judah and promise of divine intervention is exactly fulfilled: Judah goes up, and God gives the Canaanites and Perizzites into Judah's hand. It is important to notice the order here: Judah obeys and then God provides the victory. The notice of their defeating "ten thousand of them at Bezek" (v. 4) and of them defeating "the Canaanites and the Perizzites" (v. 5) is told in an almost off-hand way. The report of the military success here is clean and uncomplicated.

The mention of Israel's defeat at Bezek sets the stage for the second story in the introduction. Their capture and humiliation of the enemy Adoni-bezek (literally, in Hebrew, "The Lord of Bezek") has a quality of fantasy; the tribe of Judah captures Adoni-bezek in the town of Bezek (where else would they find him?) and cuts off his thumbs and his big toes. The unusual punishment that the people of Judah inflict upon him is explained not by a theologically heavy-handed narrator, but rather by Adoni-bezek himself. He understands why he is being punished in this strange way and says, "Seventy kings with their thumbs and big toes cut off used to pick up scraps under my table; as I have done, so God has paid me back" (1:7). Adoni-bezek does not see his punishment as being perpetrated by the vindictive Judahites, but in terms of balance, equity, rightness.

The theme of retribution is one that we will see regularly throughout the book, and one with which we will have to wrestle. We should, therefore, spend just a little time here, near the very beginning and

> *The theme of retribution is one that we will see regularly throughout the book, and one with which we will have to wrestle.*

get a handle on this difficult concept, since it will be important later. Many Christians think of retribution as an unfortunate and bloody holdover from a more theologically primitive time. And, we must admit, the way the term is used and misused by some people certainly helps to argue for this interpretation. In the theological outlook of the book of Judges, however, it is very different, and here, at the very beginning and in the mouth of a Canaanite king, we can discern that retribution is something different than a mean-spirited, vengeful response to past offenses.

The Hebrew verb that is placed in Adoni-bezek's mouth for what God has done is *shillam*, which is translated as "paid . . . back." We think of "paying someone back" for something, at least in this type of context, with responding in kind: you did something bad to me, so I will do something bad back to you. This is, for us, what "pay-back" is all about. But *shillam* comes from the same root, in fact, as the well-known Hebrew word for "peace," *shalom*. "Shalom" from a Hebrew perspective does not mean an absence of fighting, as it usually does in English, but "balance," "equity," and "equanimity." In short, when the term is used of situations or groups of people who are "at peace" it means that there is no fighting because there is no need for fighting. Everyone has what they need; no one lacks what is necessary.

Yet, in the real world, this is rare. Violent deeds, oppressive attitudes and actions, upset the balance and upend the "shalom" that should reign. And Israelite religion in almost all its aspects, as well as almost every other major religious tradition, notes that when a person or a group of people attempt to overturn the balance of reality, reality wins. Whether it is found in the Buddhist idea of karma or the Christian teaching of justice, the idea that those who perpetrate violence and oppression do not usually succeed in the long run is practically universal. And Adoni-bezek himself recognizes this. He violently humiliated others; now his own deeds have come back upon his own head—or rather his thumbs and big toes.

The story of Adoni-bezek also sets the background for the military report that follows. As they captured that enemy, so the report informs us, they defeat three other even worse foes. The tribe of Judah continues to succeed in its military incursions against

Jerusalem, in the central hills, in the desert southern region, and in the low, coastal region. They also come to the important city of Hebron and defeat the three rulers of the town, Sheshai, Ahiman, and Talmai. These names mean little to modern readers, but for ancient readers they were synonymous with almost superhuman enemies, practically undefeatable. They are mentioned, as the "sons of Anak" or "the Anakites" in Numbers 13:22–33 and in Deuteronomy 2:10–11 and 9:2, where they stand as symbols of unbeatable power. We might think of them as Godzilla, King Kong, and the Terminator. The remarkable thing here is, of course, that Judah defeats them, and that their defeat is mentioned, again, in an almost off-handed way. It seems as if Judah cannot lose for winning!

The final story in this optimistic prologue involves not only war but also love, and not only a battle but also a marriage. Generally, the flow and meaning of this little story seems clear. Caleb, a hero from the previous book of Joshua, offers his daughter, Achsah, as a prize for whoever defeats a city named Kiriath-sefer. Othniel, his nephew, defeats the city and Caleb gives him Achsah as a wife. In spite of the military character of the chapter as a whole, the taking of Kiriath-sefer is merely the setting for this story, which centers on Achsah. At the beginning she appears as only a name and an object, someone or something promised and given as a reward. She is a passive token.

But halfway through the story, Achsah becomes the primary actor. At first she tries to stay in the background, urging her new husband Othniel to ask for a particular portion of land from her father. But she cannot stay hidden. She herself takes the initiative, comes to Caleb, asks for the portion (called "Gulloth-mayim," "Watering Basins") and, instead, receives even more than she asked ("Upper Basins" and "Lower Basins"). This theme of someone who is passive, hidden, or unexpected rising to the occasion, taking initiative, and getting their way will play out over and over throughout Judges. Sometimes this turn of events will lead to Israel's advantage; very often, however, it will lead to Israel's undoing. Here at the beginning of the book, however, Achsah's story is a wholly positive one of a woman's daring rewarded.

This theme of someone who is passive or hidden rising to the occasion, taking initiative, and getting their way will play out over and over throughout Judges.

All together, the stories of Judah and Simeon, the defeat of Adoni-
bezek, and the initiative of Achsah promote a clear and hopeful tone
to this prologue to the book of Judges. The themes of cooperation,
retribution, and initiative that seemingly so easily work in Israel's
favor will not last, however. In the second half of this first prologue,
things will get both more complex and more troubling, until by the
end the Israelites will weep for their failures, both in their military
exploits but even more for their faithlessness in their relationship
with God.

If I were to organize and name this second half of the introduction, I would call it "the troubling ending" and lay out the stories
and reports in the following way:

- Story: The descendants of Hobab and human betrayal
- Report: Military success and failure
- Story: Joseph and deal-making with the enemy
- Report: Military failure
- Story: Israel weeps

Here, again, you can see the flip-flop quality of the stories and
reports. This organizational scheme causes these various small units
to cohere together to form a single section with an overarching message. One can tell, even from the titles that I have given them, these
are not stories of cooperation and victory and initiative, but rather
of betrayal and collusion and sadness. If Judges as a whole can be
thought of as tragedy, so can this initial introduction to the book.

Immediately after the story of Achsah, we are informed that,
beforehand during the exodus from Egypt, a group of non-Israelite
people also came up with Israel and settled in the general area where
the tribe of Judah lived. These people, however, migrate elsewhere
and begin to align themselves with other ethnic groups, either the
Amalekites or the Canaanites, the "people of the land." These people, who were once allies of Israel, begin to cooperate with Israel's
enemies.

There seems to be some confusion among biblical texts and biblical scholars about some aspects of this tiny story. I believe that this
confusion might be intentional; the troubling aspects of the text
actually mirror the troubling aspects of the wider story itself. It

causes the reader to pause a bit after the relatively harmonious beginning and reconsider what is going on with this story of the Israelites
and their new-found enemies. What are the troubling aspects of this
story? First, the name of the ancestor of the people is unclear, because
the Hebrew text does not include the name "Hobab"; it only appears
in early translations of the text. So, first, we are unclear as to who
these people are. Second, even if the name of the ancestor was
Hobab, his exact relationship with Moses is unclear, since most
scholars think Hobab was the "son-in-law" of Moses, rather than his
"father-in-law," who is usually called Jethro. So, whether these people ever actually were aligned with Israel is brought into question.
And third, where they eventually settle is open to question: most
ancient texts have "Amalekites," while the Hebrew text has "the people," which would be another way of naming the general inhabitants
of the land, the Canaanites. Nevertheless, the overall point of this
small story is clear. A group of non-Israelite people, who were
assumed to be allies before, have now aligned themselves with either
the Amalekites or "the people" of the land, the Canaanites.

The Amalekites were, like Sheshai, Ahiman, and Talmai, the traditional enemies of Israel. Unlike the Anakites, however, the Amalekites
were not defeated by Israel in its early taking of the land, but
remained there until at least the reign of David. The fact, therefore,
that a group closely associated with Israel would defect and support
Israel's known enemy is troubling. Questions of loyalty or betrayal
should, from this point forward, remain in our mind as we read.

The story of the defection of the people of Hobab turns naturally
into the first military report in this second half of the prologue. The
military exploits here are neither as simple or as successful as in the
beginning. Judah, true to its promise, goes with Simeon into its ter-
ritory and together the tribes win a victory at Zephath/Hormah. But
then, suddenly, the focus switches back to Judah alone and the conquest of the Philistine cities of Gaza, Ashkelon, and Ekron. What
happened to staying and helping Simeon? Does Judah, like Hobab,
desert those with whom they were allied?

Moreover, a curious little notice is inserted in 1:19: "The LORD
was with Judah and he took possession of the hill country, but could
not drive out the inhabitants of the plain, because they had chariots

of iron." How strange that God's presence with Judah is the cause of their success in the hill country, but it cannot overcome something as straightforward as iron chariots. After the defeat of the Anakites, iron chariots prove to be too much for Judah and God. Is this a bit of irony thrown in, introducing the notion that the presence of God is not simply the same thing as success? We are also told that Caleb, who was from the tribe of Judah (Numbers 13:6), was given Hebron, but then are also told that it was he who defeated the three sons of Anak. While it is a success, in this retelling it is not a success for all of Judah (as we might have thought beforehand), but only of Caleb. We are also told that the other tribe in the south, Benjamin, could not defeat the inhabitants of Jerusalem, even though the defeat of Jerusalem has already been recounted in verse 8. It seems as if the second half of this introduction portrays the undoing and under-mining of much of the success that we had assumed in the first half. Now success does not belong to the entire tribe, but only to individuals, while defeat is introduced as a possibility—even though it was assured in previous stories and, in this retelling, defeat is possible even with God's presence.

The military success of Caleb, the military stalemate of Judah, and the defeat of Benjamin provide the backdrop for the story of the taking of the city of Bethel by the "house of Joseph," a prominent coalition of Israelite tribes. This taking of the city of Bethel is, at the end of the day, a success story: the city becomes an Israelite posses-sion. But the way in which the victory is brought about is ambiguous, involving threats and deal-making. Until now the relationship between Israel and the local populace in Canaan is supposed to be clear: the Israelites are to make no agreements, deals, or covenants with any of the Canaanites (Exodus 23:32; 34:11–16). Yet here, Joseph allows a Canaanite man and his family to escape the destruction of the city.

Early on, Israel is portrayed as ambivalent and even disobe-dient while at the same time appearing to be victorious.

Is this story, as it is often discussed by some scholars, a positive example of how Israel (or, at least, Joseph) "keeps its word" in its dealing with others? Is this vignette supposed to be a success story? Perhaps, but I suspect not. It is a perfect example of how a story that is separated from its context can mean one thing, but when seen as one element within a larger plot, it can mean something else. Set as it is in the midst of a list of failures by the tribes of Israel, and in light of the condemnation that Israel will receive in the final story in this introduction, this story is meant to show Israel as ambivalent and even disobedient while simultaneously seeming victorious.

The second military report in this troubling ending of the introduction lays out a long list of military successes (which are few) and military stalemates and failures (which are many). The list of names of tribes and villages and cities throughout this section drives home the utter failure of Israel to take the land. Even the few glimpses we get of relative success—for example, the Canaanites serve the Israelites as forced labor—are overwhelmed by the constant refrain that Israel *did not drive out* this or that indigenous population.

The slow breakdown of Israel is very artfully woven into this section by short passages noting who is living with whom. Notice how the progression goes from Canaanites living throughout the land to Canaanites living in the midst of Israelites, and then to Israelites living in the midst of Canaanites:

- "The Canaanites continued to live in that land" (v. 27)
- "The Canaanites lived among [Ephraim] in Gezer" (v. 29)
- "The Canaanites lived among [Zebulun]" (v. 30)
- "The Asherites lived among the Canaanites, the inhabitants of the land" (v. 32)
- "[Naphtali] lived among the Canaanites, the inhabitants of the land" (v. 33).

It is as if, by the end, the Canaanites are the real "inhabitants of the land," with the tribes of Israel trying to find a place, here and there, to settle out of their way. This culminates, finally, in the notice that the tribe of Dan was forced back by the Amorites and was not allowed to live in its place on the plain. Although Joseph subjects the Amorites to forced labor, it seems a hollow victory, particularly for Dan. Although God had originally promised to drive out the Canaanites, it now seems that it is Israel itself that is being driven out of the land that they had not yet even conquered.

A final, sad story brings this troubling ending of the first introduction to a close. "The angel of the LORD" brings Israel the news

that the growing string of failures we have seen throughout the introduction is not tied to military might or weakness, nor is it a result of
poor planning or unfortunate circumstances. These failures are
explained theologically by the messenger:

> Now the angel of the Lord went up from Gilgal to Bochim, and said, "I
> brought you up from Egypt, and brought you into the land that I had
> promised to your ancestors. I said, 'I will never break my covenant with
> you. For your part, do not make a covenant with the inhabitants of this
> land; tear down their altars.' But you have not obeyed my command.
> See what you have done! So now I say, I will not drive them out before
> you; but they shall become adversaries to you, and their gods shall be a
> snare to you" (2:1–3).

For even though the covenantal plan was for God to give the
Israelites the land, they have not obeyed the simple two-fold command: refrain from agreements with the people of the land, and des-
ecrate their altars. In retrospect, the command does not seem so very
difficult or complex. Yet from the presence of the
descendants of Hobab, who then become associates of the Amalekites, to the deal made with the
man from Bethel, Israel seems to have always been
closely associated with the "people of the land"
and, as a result, their successes are incomplete (as
with Simeon), undone (as with Benjamin and
Jerusalem), underhanded (as with Joseph and Bethel), ambiguous
(as with Manasseh, Ephraim, Zebulun, Asher, and Naphtali), or non-
existent (as with Dan).

"So now I say, I will not drive
them out before you; but they
shall become adversaries to
you, and their gods shall be
a snare to you" (2:1–3).

The introduction finally ends with Israel responding to the report
by the angel by doing three things: they weep, they name the place
"Bochim" ("weeping" or "weepers" in Hebrew), and they offer sacrifices. The introduction ends exactly where it began, with the actions
that Israel as a whole makes toward God. What is God's response?
We are not told. The introduction suddenly ends. What would we
want God's response to be? What would be a reconciling response?
Forgiveness? Re-establishment of the covenant? We will see many
examples in Judges of how God responds to Israel with forgiveness.

But here we are left with Israel weeping and sacrificing at Bochim. The introduction that began so optimistically ends in weeping.

The Second Introduction (2:6–3:11)

The second prologue to the book of Judges falls into much larger blocks of material than the first. Whereas the earlier introduction was composed of several small stories and quick reports of military activities, the second falls into three large sections. We have the description of Israel as a faithful people, followed by an outline of the cyclical pattern of sin, oppression, deliverance, and relapse into sin that we will find in many of the stories in the middle of the book, and ending with a description of Israel's faithlessness and its assimilation into the surrounding Canaanite population.

This second prologue begins, as with the first, on a very positive, sanguine note. Looking back at the time of Joshua, it pictures Israel as a whole, faithfully following God and living in the land that it had been promised. The passage contrasts with the final chapter of Joshua, where the faithfulness of Israel is called into question by the doubts of Joshua and by his own prediction that Israel will prove to be unfaithful: "You cannot serve the Lord, for he is a holy God. He is a jealous God; he will not forgive your transgressions or your sins. If you forsake the Lord and serve foreign gods, then he will turn and do you harm, and consume you, after having done you good" (Joshua 24:19–20). Here in the second introduction to Judges, however, Israel is portrayed as faithfully worshipping God for as long as Joshua and his generation live. No doubts cloud the scene; Israel is wholesome and faithful in its relationship with God.

Unlike the beginning of the first prologue to the book of Judges, however, the death of Joshua here in the second introduction does not lead Israel to accept covenantal responsibility and turn to God for direction. No, here the deaths of Joshua and of his generation cause *another* generation that does not know God or what he had done to arise and take its place. In this pattern, the death of a leader leads to the defection of the people.

As in the first introduction, Israel acts as a whole, as a single body. Here, however, Israel's actions are not about cooperating with each other and defeating the Canaanites, but doing "what was evil in the sight of the LORD" and worshipping "the Baals," the deities of the Canaanites. The description of the sin is repetitive and long, with phrases hanging on to each other in long lines. The section begins with the double indictment, "They worshipped the Baals; and they abandoned the LORD," and ends with its inversion, "They abandoned the LORD and worshipped the Baals and the Astartes" (2:11–13).

This double phrase encapsulates what the Deuteronomists would have described as sin. Sin is, for this narrator, not simply doing bad things or, even, disobeying certain laws. Sin is less about the actions of "following other gods and bowing down to them" (2:12), than it is of living in the midst of a broken relationship with God. Living outside that relationship and outside that covenant is the essence of what sin is all about. Sin is not, however, just an ethereal state of being; it has real consequences in what one does; it affects everything else in the life of a society. And this, for the narrator in Judges, is at the heart of the tragedy of the stories that we are about to be told.

For Judges sin is less about bowing down to foreign gods than it is of living in the midst of a broken relationship with God.

The unavoidable result of Israel's sinfulness and resulting evil actions is that God undermines their success and sells them into the power of their enemies. God thwarts even their attempts to succeed, who brings "misfortune" (literally "evil") upon them. It is as if Israel's initial sin, their doing "evil" beforehand, is simply continued here, finding a fulfillment in their military attempts. The "evil" that Israel seeks and perpetrates eventually infects its future and its context. "Evil" changes; it is no longer what Israel does, but what is done to Israel. At that point, after Israel has been oppressed and plundered by enemies, God raises up a judge, a deliverer, who rescues them from their oppressors. It is important to notice, however, that this deliverance does not return Israel to a time of closeness to God as they had experienced under the leadership of Joshua. Far from it— even during the period of their deliverance the Israelites continue to be unfaithful (or, as the NRSV translates it, "to lust"; literally, "to prostitute themselves") toward God. Yet the presence of the judge assures Israel's ongoing deliverance from oppression, at least during his lifetime.

But, with the death of the judge, Israel does something unusual. The NRSV translates the sentence this way: when the judge died, "they would relapse and behave worse than their ancestors. They would not drop any of their practices or their stubborn ways" (2:19). The word "relapse" makes Israel's response sound almost accidental, whereas the actual phrasing is more in line with, "They would turn around and they would cause rottenness/spoilage/destruction more than their ancestors." In other words, Israel, left on its own without a judge, actively seeks its own ruin. Moreover, the verb "drop" near the end of the verse is important; Israel holds on tightly even to those things that should naturally "fall away" or "get left behind." Here, at the beginning of the next cycle, Israel is in a very different place than before. And as the book progresses, over and over, through each act of deliverance, the corrupting effect of Israel's sin will be seen not only upon the Israelites themselves, but also upon the judges as things go from better to worse and, eventually, to utter chaos.

As with the first introduction, this ends with God withdrawing covenantal protection from Israel. In the first prologue the loss of God's blessing provokes the people to weep at Bochim and to offer sacrifices. Here, however, at the end of the second introduction, the picture is much bleaker. After we are given a long list of the indigenous people remaining in the land, we are told that it is God himself who is allowing these groups to remain, in order to see if Israel would "walk in the way of the LORD as their ancestors did" (2:22). Israel, however, is not up to the challenge. By the end of this second introduction, Israel as a whole is intermarrying with the Canaanites, essentially becoming one with them, and worshipping their gods.

As I said before, the first thing we come upon in any literary work is extremely important. The two introductions of Judges provide us with clues as to what we can expect for the rest of the book. The first hints that the story will be a slow slide from relative happiness and prosperity to relative chaos and uncertainty. After reading it we will expect that the book of Judges as a whole will not end happily, but are intrigued about how this slow slide will progress and what will bring it about. The second prologue suggests that Judges will unfold by means of a series of smaller stories, each having a similar outline. Through each individual story's retelling of Israel's sin, its oppression by enemies, its deliverance by a military judge, and its eventual relapse into sin, through the build-up of story after story, we expect these individual scenes and stories to be a cycle, whereby Israel repeats the tragedy over and over.

By combining the slow slide downward of the first introduction with the cyclical pattern of the second introduction, we expect the rest of the book of Judges to be a downward spiral, whereby each story of sin, oppression, deliverance, and relapse leads further and further toward the book's—and Israel's—end. But, in order for the slide to be from contentment to wretchedness, we must begin with a story of relative simplicity and hope. And so we do, turning to the story of Othniel in the following chapter.

CHAPTER THREE

Faithfulness and Fickleness: Othniel to Gideon

Patterns, whether they are repetitions of images, phrases, or types of characters, are very important whenever people tell or write stories. That is why good writers often repeat similar types of scenes or exact or similar words while constructing their plots; it gives valuable hints to the reader about what he or she might reasonably expect for future scenes. The mention of a revolver lying behind the clock on the mantel, and a repeated mention of it later in a murder mystery, is probably a signal that the revolver will somehow be important for the plot at some future time. The repeated mention of a character's fear of heights suggests that the character will deal with that fear later in the story. Authors rarely spend time or energy introducing and then later reintroducing an object, or a characteristic, or even an unusual word or phrase for no reason. The repetition is meant to heighten the reader's expectations about how the story will continue and, perhaps, reach its end.

Yet it is not only repetitions in stories that are important. Equally important is how a pattern that is introduced is "broken" in order to provide suspense or to lead to a surprise. I like to tell a slightly revised version of "The Three

Little Pigs" to show how patterns often work in stories, even relatively simple stories.

> Once upon a time, three little pigs went out into the world to make their way. The first little pig built his house out of straw. The second little pig built his house out of sticks. The third little pig built his house out of bricks.
>
> One day, the big bad wolf came to the straw house of the first little pig. He said, "Little pig, little pig, let me in!" The pig replied, "Not by the hair of my chinny-chin-chin!" To which the wolf threatened, "Then I'll huff and I'll puff and I'll blow your house in!" And he did, and he ate the pig!
>
> Then the next day, the big bad wolf came to the stick house of the second little pig. He said, "Little pig, little pig, let me in!" The pig replied, "Not by the hair of my chinny-chin-chin!" To which the wolf threatened, "Then I'll huff and I'll puff and I'll blow your house in!" And he did, and he ate the pig!
>
> Then the next day, the big bad wolf came to the brick house of the third little pig. He said, "Little pig, little pig, let me in!" The pig replied, "Not by the hair of my chinny-chin-chin!" To which the wolf threatened, "Then I'll huff and I'll puff and I'll blow your house in!" And he did, and he ate the pig!

This version of the story shows a vital point about storytelling: patterns are important, but sometimes the point of the pattern is for it to be broken. The ending of the story as it stands in this version is a let-down, and not just for the three little pigs. We can easily recognize the pattern of the story, with its similar phrasing ("Little pig, little pig," "chinny-chin-chin," "And he did, and he ate the pig!"), as well as the threefold repetition of the variable parts of the story ("first . . . second . . . third," "straw . . . sticks . . . bricks"). But because this version of the story relies so closely upon the pattern, the plot fizzles at the end. In the original version of the story, the third little pig survives and turns the tables on the wolf because the point of the story's pattern is for it to be broken.

In the last chapter we saw that the book of Judges is introduced in a couple of ways that provide a hint at where the story will go in future chapters. The first introduction provides a linear chronicle in which

Israel descends from a time of harmonious com-
monality and close relationship with both itself and
with God, through a time of occasional failure,
only to end in impotence and chaos. The second
introduction, on the other hand, provides a more
"pattern-driven" perspective—Israel's relationship
with God goes through a cycle made up of the stages of sin, oppression, deliverance, peace until the death of the judge, and then
another relapse into sin. Together they give the impression of a
descending spiral, where each round of the pattern draws Israel
closer and closer to anarchy.

Israel's relationship with God is a cycle of sin, oppression, deliverance, peace until the death of the judge, and then another relapse into sin.

Throughout the following judge stories, we will want to be particularly aware of the patterns that have been so carefully introduced by
those editors who crafted this book into its final form. We will see that
the slow, descending line from Israel's relatively stable society at the
beginning of the stories down to the utter disorder at their end will,
more or less, be a constant theme throughout. The cyclical pattern
will, however, begin to fracture fairly early in the series, but as the stories progress, the pattern will grow less and less predictable. This slow
disintegration of the pattern will be paralleled in the common life of
Israel itself, as well as in the lives of the judges whom God raises up.

Othniel, the Perfect Judge (3:7–11)

The judge stories begin with Othniel. I describe Othniel as the "perfect" judge because his story follows the pattern of the second introduction so closely. Even a casual reader of the second introduction to
Judges cannot help but see how the story of Othniel directly follows
the pattern that has been laid down. As described in the previous
chapter, the story falls, almost naturally, into the four-fold outline:

> The Israelites did what was evil in the sight of the LORD.
>
> The anger of the LORD was kindled against Israel, and he sold them
> into the hand of King Cushan-rishathaim of Aram-naharaim.
>
> But when the Israelites cried out to the LORD, the LORD raised up a
> deliverer for the Israelites, who delivered them, Othniel son of Kenaz.
>
> So the land had rest forty years. Then Othniel son of Kenaz died.

The storyline is so simple and straightforward, following the pattern so closely, that it seems as if little needs to be said about it. However, since this story repeats the pattern of the second introduction—a pattern that will soon be breaking apart—I want to spend a little extra time on Othniel's story. Although it is the shortest of the true judge stories, it is, in a way, the most important of them all. Before turning to the next judge, therefore, I want to point out a few important details in the story that provide a foundation for the pattern that will both appear and disintegrate in the stories that come after Othniel.

SIN

Although I call this episode in the pattern "sin," the actual term that appears here and elsewhere in Judges is the phrase "to do evil in the sight of the LORD." This phrase, used in the second introduction to describe Israel's apostasy, will also be used again and again throughout the following stories, usually at their opening, which will signal the beginning of a new cycle.

Additionally, the phrase "to worship the Baals and the Asherahs" was also used twice in the second introduction to describe the "sin" episode and once, right before the Othniel story, to describe the resumption of Israel's sinning. The verb "to worship" in the phrase is, actually, the verb "to serve" in Hebrew (*avad*). The fact that the Israelites not only "do evil" in God's eyes but also "serve" foreign gods will be an important point tying this episode with the next.

OPPRESSION

Since the Israelites "serve" the gods and goddesses of the Canaanites, God hands them over to a Canaanite king, Cushan-rishathaim from Aram-naharaim, or Syria. Furthermore, since the Israelites want to "serve" (that is, worship) foreign gods, they must also "serve" Cushan-rishathaim, which they do for eight years.

This is an important point for appreciating the concept of "punishment" in the Old Testament as well as in the New Testament. There is a common assumption that God punishes the sinner in some sort of supernatural and cataclysmic way. If someone sins, then God strikes them dead with a bolt of lightning or punishes them with a plague of frogs. And while, it must be admitted, there are some cases where it rains for forty days and forty nights, as at the time of Noah, or swarms of locusts suddenly appear and destroy the land, as in Exodus, these sorts of punishments are relatively rare.

Much more common is the notion that punishment comes directly from the unhealthy or unhelpful or destructive nature of the sin itself. Thus Amos decries the sin of the ruling class in ancient Israel by noting that they are oppressing poor people in order to gain exorbitant wealth and lie on "couches of ivory," and predicts that their wealth itself will so weigh them down when a foreign enemy invades that they will not be able to escape. Or Ezekiel notes that Judah's sin is so bad that it is corrupting the very land where people are living, and predicts that a time will come that dead bodies will lie out in the open because the ground will no longer be able to receive them. The oppression which Israel suffers, in other words, is not something completely foreign to their experience. Their punishment is simply the fulfillment of their sin; the oppression is the result of their sin "writ large."

> *Much more common in the Hebrew Bible is the notion that punishment comes directly from the unhealthy or unhelpful or destructive nature of the sin itself.*

This is the case, as we will see, throughout the book of Judges. If Israel wants to serve foreign deities, then Israel will also serve a foreign ruler. The punishment not only fits the crime; it actually *is* the crime in another guise.

DELIVERANCE

Two points should be noticed in the way the story relates the deliverance of Israel by Othniel. First, deliverance comes not simply as God's clear-cut response to Israel's oppression, but rather because Israel "cries out" to the LORD. While not an isolated episode, the theme of Israel crying out to God is rare. It will appear again in the story of Ehud as well as in a major turning point in the book later on—the description of the oppression under the Ammonites, right before the raising up of Jephthah. The appearance of Israel "crying out" against oppression here sets the stage for those two other scenes, and this repetition will be especially important for understanding the message of the book as a whole.

Another detail to notice here is that Othniel accomplishes the deliverance through some sort of spiritual, charismatic experience, described as "the spirit of the LORD came upon him." While again the action of God's spirit is not so common in the book as to constitute a separate "episode" in the cycle, it will appear again in the story of Gideon and the story of Jephthah, as well as several times in the story of the final judge, Samson. Particularly since this theme appears here, in the first judge story, as well as in the last, we will want to pay special attention to how the repetition of the activity of the "spirit of the LORD" works in those other stories. Does the theme continue the pattern of equipping the judge to deliver Israel from oppression, or does it break the pattern by doing something else? We shall see.

PEACE UNTIL THE DEATH OF THE JUDGE

The last verse of the story describes the final episode in the cycle. In the second introduction, this part of the pattern was described as "[God] delivered them from the hand of their enemies all the days of the judge. . . . But whenever the judge died, they would relapse." Beginning here, at the end of the first judge story, this episode is described using a very unusual phrase, particularly as it reads in Hebrew: "the land had rest." The word for "peace" here is not the usual one known by most people, which is "shalom." Instead, the word used here—*shaqat*—implies "quietness" or "not being disturbed," and we see it most often in poetry.[10] It is an unusual word to appear here, somewhat like the relatively rare English words "quietude" and "placidity," both of which sound more like poetry than telling a story.

> *The word for "peace" here is not shalom but shaqat, which implies "quietness" or "not being disturbed."*

The sentence, "The land had quietude for XX years," is one of the most frequently used phrases in the first half of the book of Judges. Along with its appearance here with Othniel, it also rounds out the stories of Ehud, Deborah, and Gideon. It is missing from the stories of Jephthah and Samson, which gives some indication of the "disquietude" in the latter half of the book.

Ehud, the Resourceful Judge (3:12–30; 4:1)

The beginning of the story of Ehud is almost identical with the pattern we have been discussing in the story of Othniel. Furthermore, when the beginning of the story of Ehud is combined with its final verse (v. 30), the storyline is essentially the same as Othniel's:

> The Israelites again did what was evil in the sight of the LORD (v. 12a);

> and the LORD strengthened King Eglon of Moab against Israel, because they had done what was evil in the sight of the LORD. In alliance with the Ammonites and the Amalekites, he went and defeated Israel; and they took possession of the city of palms. So the Israelites served King Eglon of Moab eighteen years (vv. 12b–14).

> But when the Israelites cried out to the LORD, the LORD raised up for them a deliverer, Ehud son of Gera, the Benjaminite (v. 15).

> . . . So Moab was subdued that day under the hand of Israel. And the land had rest eighty years (v. 30).

Two main differences appear between the story of Othniel and the story of Ehud. The most obvious difference, of course, is the much longer "deliverance episode" in the Ehud story. Instead of simply telling about the victory of Israel over King Eglon of Moab, its oppressor—as in the Othniel cycle—the narrator here becomes much more expansive in the two-part story about how Ehud won the victory over Moab.

In the first part, through deception and using the rare attribute of his left-handedness, Ehud is able to kill the king, Eglon. The assassination of the king is told in a fairly humorous manner, at least to its original audience. The king is presented as highly gullible, willing to be left alone with one of his downtrodden ambassadors. His name itself, as well as his size and weight, are likewise ironic: "Eglon" comes from the Semitic word for "calf" (*'egel*); so it is that Ehud kills the "fatted calf" in anticipation of his victory. Finally, the story is filled with what might be called "bathroom humor"; the king's associates do not find his corpse until much later because they believe that he was "relieving himself in the cool chamber" (3:24). The majority of this first part, therefore, is devoted to the killing of the Moabite king.

In the second part of the deliverance episode, the story then quickly traces the rallying of the Israelites and the routing of the Moabites. This portion of the story is straightforward, with little complication, and ends with the killing of "ten thousand Moabites, all strong, able-bodied men." The victory is quick, decisive and, it seems, without any Israelite casualties.

The primary difference, therefore, between the stories of Othniel and Ehud is the expansion of the "deliverance episode" in Ehud's story. The second difference is less easy to see, particularly in the New Revised Standard Version translation, but is, in several ways, as important as the expansion of the deliverance. For the ending of the Ehud story actually breaks the pattern in a couple of ways. Based upon the order established in the second introduction and continued in the Othniel story, we would reasonably guess that the Ehud story should end this way:

> So Moab was subdued that day under the hand of Israel. And the land had rest eighty years. Then Ehud the son of Gera died.

And this notice of Ehud's death would naturally be followed by a statement about Israel sinning again. This is not, however, what we have. Instead, the end of the Ehud story ends this way:

> So Moab was subdued that day under the hand of Israel. And the land had rest eighty years. After him came Shamgar son of Anath, who killed six hundred of the Philistines with an oxgoad. He too delivered Israel. The Israelites again did what was evil in the sight of the LORD, after Ehud died (3:30–4:1).

First, there is a second "savior," Shamgar, who is unexpectedly inserted at the end of the Ehud cycle, whom we will quickly look at in the next section. Second, and even more telling, is the first verse of chapter four. The NRSV translators, obviously being strongly influenced by the pattern, have the notice of Ehud's death inserted as a dependent clause ("after Ehud died"), treating his death almost as an afterthought. In Hebrew, however, Ehud's death stands in an independent clause ("Now, Ehud had died" or "Now, Ehud was dead"). This change confuses the order. Israel is now sinning, and Ehud is now dead. But which came first and which came second, Israel's apostasy or Ehud's death? Instead of the straight-forward and simple statement about the quiet of the land, followed by the notice of the death of the judge, followed by the statement about the sinning of Israel, Ehud's story ends ambiguously.[11] The effect is subtle, but the ramifications for the slight

The pattern established so carefully in the prologue and repeated, almost word for word, in the story of Othniel is already starting to fray.

change are—or will come to be—momentous. The pattern established so carefully in the second introduction and repeated, almost word for word, in the story of Othniel is already starting to fray.

Shamgar, the Marginal Judge

The story of Shamgar brings another slight change in the pattern, because all we have is the deliverance episode— "After him came Shamgar son of Anath, who killed six hundred of the Philistines with an ox-goad. He too delivered Israel" (3:31). There is no notice about Israel sinning, about God becoming angry and giving them into the hands of the Philistines, about them crying out under their oppressors, or about God raising up a judge to deliver Israel. Nor are we told about the land having quietness after his deliverance, nor about his death. Even though most of these are simply formulaic elements that could have easily been inserted before and after Shamgar's story of deliverance, the compilers of the book of Judges do not include them. We are simply told about the victory that he won against six hundred Philistines through unusual means, like Ehud (and Jael, Gideon, and Samson later in the book). We have only a single verse, a single part of the pattern, so that Shamgar and his remarkable victory almost seems like a postscript, tucked into the end of Ehud's story.

Deborah, the Disappearing Judge (4:4–5:31)

The cyclical pattern that was begun in the second introduction continued in the stories of Othniel and Ehud, begins to collapse utterly in the story of Deborah. The cycle begins clearly and strongly, eventually ending with the formula of the land resting, which we have come to expect:

> The Israelites again did what was evil in the sight of the LORD. Ehud was dead (4:1).

So the LORD sold them into the hand of King Jabin of Canaan, who reigned in Hazor; the commander of his army was Sisera, who lived in Harosheth-ha-goiim. Then the Israelites cried out to the LORD for help; for he had nine hundred chariots of iron, and had oppressed the Israelites cruelly twenty years (4:2–3).

At that time Deborah, a prophetess, wife of Lappidoth, was judging Israel. She used to sit under the palm of Deborah between Ramah and Bethel in the hill country of Ephraim; and the Israelites came up to her for judgment . . . (4:4ff).

And the land had rest forty years. (5:31).

What is different here? The pattern in the story of Deborah is obviously changed by expanding the deliverance episode, as in the Ehud story, but the expansion makes it a far more complicated story. Here, the deliverance episode includes a complex series of episodes:

- Deborah and Barak negotiating the conduct of the war against the Canaanites.
- The migration of Heber the Kenite away from the rest of his family.
- The meeting of the Canaanite and Israelite armies, the victory of Israel, and the escape of Sisera, the Canaanite general.
- The murder of Sisera by Jael, the wife of Heber the Kenite.
- A short notice about the deliverance.
- A long and ancient poem of victory, placed in the mouths of Deborah and Barak.

The complexity of these texts reflects the fact that they probably each had an independent life long before the book of Judges was compiled. In their final form, as we have it here, they work with each other to produce a wonderful story, full of suspense and narrative tension.

In the scene of the negotiations between Deborah and Barak, the latter seems like an unlikely hero. Deborah, who is making judicial decisions for Israel, summons him and gives him an oracle: "Go to Mount Tabor with the army . . . and I will give Sisera into your hand." Barak, however, seems reluctant to obey, and gives Deborah an ultimatum that he will only go if she goes with him. She agrees, but his reticence leads to his own loss of glory: now, Deborah declares, the victory will be given into a woman's hand instead. We naturally believe—because she is a "judge," she seems to be the one taking the initiative, she is the one in contact with God, and it is she who is drawing up the battle plans—that she, herself, will win the victory. We will have to wait to see if our expectations are fulfilled, if Deborah is the one who delivers.

> *"At that time Deborah, a prophetess, wife of Lappidoth, was judging Israel. She used to sit under the palm of Deborah between Ramah and Bethel in the hill country of Ephraim."*

The short notice about the migration of Heber the Kenite seems out of place. What, we might ask, does this have to do with anything having to do with the story of Deborah and Barak? Perhaps Heber will be the one they will fight? Perhaps Heber's family will get in the way? At this point in the story it is not clear why this little verse is included at all. We will also have to wait to see what this is about.

The actual battle takes relatively little space in the story of the deliverance of Israel. Sisera, who is the general of the opposing army, pursues the Israelite army at Mount Tabor with his own army and their chariots of iron. Barak, on the other hand, is still reluctant. Deborah must, again, tell him what to do: "Get up! This is the day that the LORD has given Sisera into your hand! The LORD is going before you!" So, now, the victory will not come about by a "woman's hand," but by Barak's. Why the change? Barak, it seems, will not proceed with the battle unless he receives the credit for defeating the Canaanite general. At first he is reticent; then, once he is assured by Deborah that God will use *him* to achieve the victory, Barak alone descends Mount Tabor with his army. The battle report is only two verses long: God confuses the Canaanite army, Sisera flees, and the army is completely wiped out. Sisera, however, is not given into Barak's hand. Will he escape completely? Again, we will have to wait to see!

Sisera flees to Heber's camp, assuming he is safe because of their alliance. Jael, Heber's wife, meets Sisera and agrees to hide him from anyone who may come looking for him. In great detail (particularly in light of the quick telling of the previous battle), the narrator notes how Jael takes on an almost maternal role with Sisera, covering him under a blanket, giving him warm milk to drink, staying nearby to protect him. But then, suddenly and unexpectedly, she nails his head to the ground while he sleeps. All that remains is for her to show Sisera to Barak, whose victory over the Canaanite general was, indeed, brought about by the hand of a woman.

At this point, all the questions of the story are resolved and it ends with a summation about the victory over the Canaanites (vv. 23–24). Who, however, brings the victory? Who, exactly, is the deliverer in his story? The story never says that "God raised up" anyone to deliver Israel, so who is in charge? Is it Deborah? Barak? Jael? All three? The summation simply says that "on that day God subdued King Jabin of Canaan before the Israelites." Although this cycle is attributed to Deborah, she—like everyone else—plays a supportive role. In a sense, God is the delivering judge in this story.

And then, unexpectedly again, Deborah and Barak break out into a song, one of the oldest in the entire Hebrew Bible:

Lord, when you went out from Seir,
when you marched from the region of Edom,
the earth trembled,
and the heavens poured,
the clouds indeed poured water.
The mountains quaked before the Lord, the One of Sinai,
before the Lord, the God of Israel. (5:4–5)

Its language, style, and images all seem to tie it to a very early period in Israel's history. The song itself is composed of smaller movements, including a general song of praise for Deborah's action and a section praising Deborah, Barak, and those tribes who aided the battle, as well reprimanding those who did not and cursing Meroz—an otherwise unknown clan or town—for not helping in the battle. The ancient song blesses Jael for her murder of Sisera, and describes Sisera's mother looking out her chamber window, wondering why her son has not yet returned from battle:

Out of the window she peered,
the mother of Sisera gazed through the lattice:
"Why is his chariot so long in coming?
Why tarry the hoofbeats of his chariots?"(5:28)

We can see from this that the Deborah cycle holds onto the pattern in most of its parts. On the other hand, however, it also distorts the pattern not only by expanding the deliverance episode, but also by removing any particular judge from the starring role. By the end of chapter 5, we are becoming uncomfortably aware that judges are not strictly necessary to bring about deliverance. The story of Deborah, Barak, and Jael raises many questions and then answers them. But it also raises an important question in its conclusion: Will God continue to raise up judges? And, if so, for what purpose? Will they continue to "deliver" Israel? Or will they have another role? We will have to see.

Gideon, the Fearful Judge (6:1–8:32a)

The long story of Gideon and Israel's victory over the Midianites begins with the usual pattern, and the basic outline of the parts of the cycle can still be discerned:

> The Israelites did what was evil in the sight of the LORD (6:1a)
>
> and the LORD gave them into the hand of Midian seven years (6:1b).
>
> When the Israelites cried to the LORD on account of the Midianites (6:3a). . . .
>
> the spirit of the LORD took possession of Gideon (6:34a).
>
> So Midian was subdued before the Israelites, and they lifted up their heads no more (8:28a).
>
> So the land had rest forty years in the days of Gideon (8:28b).
>
> Then Gideon son of Joash died at a good old age (8:32a).

While the basic pattern is still present, notice how scattered the various parts are! No longer do we have a tight block of material that contains the whole of an episode. The different formulas that we saw so clearly in the stories of Othniel and Ehud, and still remained at the beginning of the Deborah/Barak story, are separating and being expanded—and not only in the deliverance episode. Every part, with the exception of the very first episode (which is greatly reduced to just a few words), is longer and more complex. With Gideon's story we can clearly see how the complication of the pattern is paralleled in both the multifaceted view of Israel itself and in the ambiguous portrayal of its deliverer, Gideon.

The first thing that strikes us when we read this cycle (having the previous cycles in mind) is the greatly expanded episode of Israel's oppression. Up to this point, we have been told that Israel's oppression by the foreign powers has included "serving Cushan-Rishataim" of Syria eight years, or having the "City of Palms" taken away from them and serving King Eglon of Moab eighteen years, or being oppressed "cruelly" by King Jabin of Canaan twenty years. Notice the increasing length of the time of oppression in each case. In Gideon's story, however, the oppression only lasts seven years, but the narrator goes into great detail about what it involved: Israelites being forced from their homes to live in caves and strongholds, raids which destroy the crops and livestock of Israel, and overpopulation by the invading forces, which further destroy the land.

When we come to the familiar phrase, "When the Israelites cried to the LORD on account of the Midianites," we naturally believe that God's response will be to raise up a deliverer. The cycle, however, overturns our expectations; instead God sends a prophet to indict Israel for its faithlessness in forsaking its relationship with God. The judgment ends ominously:

> "Thus says the LORD, the God of Israel: I led you up from Egypt, and brought you out of the house of slavery; and I delivered you from the hand of the Egyptians, and from the hand of all who oppressed you, and drove them out before you, and gave you their land; and I said to you, 'I am the LORD your God; you shall not pay reverence to the gods of the Amorites, in whose land you live.' But you have not given heed to my voice" (6:8b–10).

What will God's response actually be? Will God forsake Israel, which we have reason to suspect from the second introduction to the book? At this point, it is not clear.

The "deliverance" episode turns our attention, instead, to the angel of God who, before, delivered a withering judgment against Israel. Here, however, he visits a frightened, cowering young man named Gideon. Unlike the Deborah/Barak story, which had no clear hero or heroine, it is clear here that Gideon is the main character of this cycle. The story, however, never directly says that God "raises up" Gideon, as we have heard in previous stories. This is perhaps because the "raising up" of Gideon takes so long; Gideon does not want to deliver Israel because of his fear. From the time that the angel initially calls Gideon to the time that he begins to fight the Midianites, twenty-two verses intervene, during which time Gideon puts off his call (and Israel's deliverance) by discussing his unworthiness ("I am the least in my family"), asking for signs and reassurances, presenting offerings, making prayers, building an altar, spending a great deal of time destroying his father's Baal shrine, and then hiding out. All this time, Israel remains under the Midianites.

Finally, Gideon is moved by the spirit and begins the offensive by rallying troops from his own clan of the Abiezrites. But then he also calls out troops from his whole tribe of Manasseh, and after that from the neighboring tribes of Asher, Zebulun, and Naphtali. Three separate calls, all the time increasing his army. Why? In light of what we know about Gideon, it is probably because he is fearful and is trying to buy time before he attacks. However, instead of directly attacking and delivering Israel, he reverts to his old ploy of asking for two different signs, each of which must occur at night. This means that he delays at least three more days before moving. Finally, his ploy of multiplying this troop base is countered by God's own instructions: the thirty-two thousand troops accompanying Gideon have to be reduced. This troop reduction—which never should have been necessary in the first place—means, of course, that Gideon has successfully bought himself even more time in reducing the troops to three hundred men.

With this out of the way, we expect Gideon to defeat the Midianite army. But, no. Gideon still fears going into battle and has to be reassured by yet another sign. That night he hears that the Midianites fear him so much that they interpret any dream at all as proof of Gideon's invincibility. This emboldens Gideon enough to set about defeating the Midianites at last, which occurs largely by their own fault because they panic. As with the story of Deborah and Barak, the military leaders escape and must be pursued. Gideon calls the tribe of Ephraim to blockade the escape routes at the waterways, which they do, and successfully capture and behead the Midianite generals, Oreb and Zeeb. As with the previous cycle, however, the expected deliverer does not actually defeat the leader of the opposing army.

While pursuing the kings of Midian, Gideon must also deal with three different factions of Israelites who are against him. For the first time in the book, we see that the delivering judge is not really in control of all of Israel, but has opponents within the nation. First, the Ephraimites are upset that they were not included in the initial attack on Midian and have to be appeased. Next he threatens the city of Succoth, whose inhabitants refuse to give him and his troops any food because, it seems, they have no confidence that he can actually win the victory against the Midianite kings. After threatening them Gideon continues on his way, only to run up against the inhabitants of Penuel who, like those in Succoth, doubt his ability.

After capturing the kings, Zebah and Zalmunna, Gideon returns to Succoth. By reverting to the same plot that we saw Israel use against the inhabitants of the Canaanite city of Luz at the very beginning of the book, he gains access to the city and tortures the officials and elders of the city mercilessly. Proceeding to Penuel, he destroys its watchtower and kills all the men of the city. When it comes to killing the Midianite kings, he tries to rely on his firstborn son to do the deed for him. Gideon's son, however, resembles his father; he is afraid. The narrator here makes an oblique insult: the son is afraid, but he is "still a boy." There is no such excuse for Gideon, and the Midianite kings even taunt him for his cowardice. Pushed to the edge, finally, Gideon kills the Midianite kings and delivers Israel.

Deliverance finally won, we expect the story to proceed to the next episode in the pattern, "peace until the death of the judge." But here, again, the story thwarts our expectations. One final scene plays out before the curtain falls on Gideon and the first half of the book. The people ask Gideon to set up a monarchy with himself and his descendants as the rulers. Gideon refuses this, perhaps in light of how kings have fared not only in his own story but also previously in the book.

He does, nevertheless, ask a gift (perhaps tribute?) from the Israelites in the form of golden earrings they had taken from the Midianites. They reply, "We will give them willingly!" This echoes the earlier song of Deborah, in which Israel and its leaders gave themselves willingly in order to win freedom from their oppressors. Here, with Gideon, the Israelites "willingly give" not themselves, but golden earrings as tribute to a non-king.

> At the end of the Gideon cycle, it is the delivering judge himself who causes Israel to sin and lays the snare for his own household.

The mention of "giving golden earrings" is an allusion to one of the most famous scenes in the Pentateuch. In Exodus 32, Aaron tells the Israelites to give him the golden earrings they wore in their ears and he models them into the form of a golden calf, which they then bow down to and worship. While Moses is up on Mount Sinai receiving the Ten Commandments and the Law, the Israelites are simultaneously worshipping an idol. This becomes one of the best-known illustrations in the Bible of Israel's faithlessness and lack of commitment to God.

When, therefore, Gideon asks the Israelites for their golden earrings, we expect a similar thing to happen—and, in this case, it does. Our expectations are, unfortunately, perfectly fulfilled. He uses the gold to create a cultic object, places it in his own hometown, and Israel "prostituted themselves to it there, and it became a snare to Gideon and to his family." We were warned earlier, in the first introduction, that the Canaanite gods would become a "snare" to Israel. How ironic that, at the end of the Gideon cycle, it is the delivering judge himself that causes Israel to sin and that lays the snare for his own household.

The long Gideon cycle draws to a close by noting that Midian "lifted up their head no more. So the land had rest for forty years in the days of Gideon" (8:28). These statements seem to be a rather hollow assurance in light of all we have been through—Israel's long oppression by the Midianites; the fear and cowardice of the judge sent to deliver Israel; the wasted time calling up and then reducing troops, thus extending Israel's humiliation; the cruel vengeance exacted upon fellow-Israelites in Succoth and Penuel; the setting up of the apostate cult in Ophrah. Yes, the Midianites were defeated and the land, at the end of the story, "had rest." But at what cost? At this point in the book, Othniel seems a far-distant memory, a time when it was clear who was good and who was bad, who was the enemy and who was "us." As the formal pattern of the story begins to disintegrate, so has Israel and so has the quality of her deliverers. Although the book is only halfway done, it is clear that the tragedy of the book of Judges is slowly sliding into chaos.

CHAPTER FOUR

The Downward Spiral: Abimelech to Samson

In one of his most famous books, *Either/Or*, the nineteenth-century philosopher Soren Kierkegaard, tells a parable about the end of the world:

> In a theater, it happened that a fire started offstage. The clown came out to tell the audience. They thought it was a joke and applauded. He told them again, and they became still more hilarious. This is the way, I suppose, that the world will be destroyed—amid the universal hilarity of wits and wags who think it is all a joke.[12]

Throughout this study I've mentioned that the book of Judges is organized like a tragedy, moving from a time of relative success and simplicity to a time of utter failure and confusion. The progression (or, rather, regression) of the overall plot of the book follows the slow disintegration of the foundational outline found in the two prologues to Judges, as well as in the short tale of the first of its judges, Othniel.

Thus far in the book of Judges we have met several deliverers of Israel. Othniel is portrayed as the best. The rest—Ehud, Deborah, Barak, Jael, and Gideon—are shown to be progressively less and less admirable, while still playing the part of the deliverers of Israel from their oppression. Israel itself becomes less and less faithful to God and the covenant, turning back and worshipping the Canaanite gods whenever they get a chance.

From this point forward in the book, as the judges/deliverers become even worse, their characters will appear almost comical. These morally bankrupt warriors will reveal weaknesses that are overblown to the point of appearing hilarious. From the ambitions of Abimelech, to the wheeling-and-dealing Jephthah, to the amorous and playful Samson, these stories will be, on a certain level, fun to read. It is no wonder that, almost forty years ago, I first heard about the book of Judges through the escapades of Samson, that slightly dim-witted strong man. Seen as characters in themselves, these judges appear comical.

But, seen from the perspective of the book as a whole, they are anything but funny. We will see them to be playing parts that are less "role models" and more as prototypes and representatives of the faithlessness and fickleness of Israel as a whole. And this moral slide toward irrelevance will be accomplished both by their own individual failings as well as by the continued brokenness of the pattern of sin, deliverance, peace, and subsequent sin that we've seen over and over thus far.

Abimelech, the Oppressive King (Judges 9)

The end of the Gideon story relates three different events, all of which serve as a backdrop for the following story of Abimelech. First, after his victory over the Midianites, the Israelites come to Gideon and ask him to set up a dynasty so that he and his son and his grandson may, in turn, rule over them. Gideon, however, refuses the offer: "I will not rule over you, and my son will not rule over you; the LORD will rule over you" (8:23). Gideon appears to be theologically faithful to God, not wanting to take the place of the LORD in ruling over Israel.

So far, well and good. In the second place, however, he asks Israel for the golden earrings that they had taken from the Midianites as the spoils of war. The Israelites are willing to give them, as well as the other spoils of war that they had seized during their battles. But now

Gideon takes the gold and makes a religious artifact to place in his own hometown of Ophrah. This object, however, becomes "a snare" to the people of Israel, who worship it, turning away from their worship of God.

Gideon takes the Midianites' gold earrings and makes a religious artifact to place in his own hometown of Ophrah.

Although the phrase "So the land had rest for forty years in the days of Gideon" *should* be immediately followed by the sentence "And Gideon died," we are told one more additional fact before Gideon leaves this life and the book. His extensive family is mentioned, including the seventy sons that he has because of his many wives in the town of Ophrah, as well as the one son, Abimelech, whom he has by his concubine, who lives in Shechem. After tracing his extensive family, Gideon's death is finally recorded.

These three facts in the conclusion of Gideon's story reveal the uneasiness with both the end of the Gideon story and the beginning of the next story of Abimelech. On the one hand, Gideon seems to inspire faithfulness by his refusal to accept kingly power, in order that God may remain Israel's true king. Yet, at the same time, he causes Israel to sin through the illicit religious object he fashioned. Furthermore he has a son whom he names "Abimelech," which means "My father is king." Thus Gideon on the one hand seems to inspire faithfulness by refusing political power, while simultaneously provoking Israel's faithlessness and, through his son Abimelech ("My father is king"), hinting that he wants a political dynasty.

Gideon's son is named "Abimelech," meaning "My father is king."

Immediately after Gideon's death, just as we would expect, Israel reverts back to their fickle lifestyle, forgetting both God and the family of Gideon. Thus far, the cyclical pattern of deliverance, and peace, followed by the death of the judge and subsequent sin holds, even in spite of the other uneasy problems just mentioned. The following story, however, is not about a judge at all, but about evil king Abimelech, Gideon's son.

On the whole, scholars are tentative as to the reason why the story of Abimelech is included in the book of Judges, since Abimelech is not a judge, nor does a judge appear anywhere in his story. The usual pattern of sin, oppression, and deliverance does not seem to be present in the story, at least in the way that it has appeared in the previous cycles. And, furthermore, none of the minor themes that we've seen—such as the spirit of God inspiring a warrior-deliverer, or the land "having rest" at the end of the story—appear in the chapter. In fact, if the story of Jephthah immediately followed that of Gideon, the cyclical pattern would hold together much better than it does with the insertion of Abimelech's story. The latter seems jarring and interrupts the pattern. What, then, is this story doing in Judges?

The problem, I think, is not in or with the story itself, but in our expectations of what the story should be. We expect the story to focus on a savior for Israel, as we have seen in the past, and we look for it to follow closely the pattern established beforehand, particularly in formulaic quotations like "the LORD sold them into the hand," "the LORD raised up for them a deliverer," or "the land had rest. . . ." But just because these exact phrases are not present in the story does not mean that the pattern isn't present.

At the end of Judges 8, we are told that, after the death of Gideon, Israel relapses and sins against God by worshipping the Canaanite Baal gods. What do we expect will happen next? Surely God will oppress Israel by placing them under the power of a cruel king. And what will be the response of God to this oppression? Surely God will rescue Israel from their oppression by using a deliverer. And, if the pattern continues, this deliverer will be an unlikely hero. What will be the outcome of the deliverance from the oppression? Surely, the land will return to a state of peace for the foreseeable future.

This is, precisely, the storyline of Judges 9, the story of Abimelech. All of these elements are present in the story, but none of the stock phrases that we have seen before occur. At the end of chapter 8 the pattern begins again, but in the transition to chapter 9, it is as if we step through the looking-glass. Our focus in this chapter is not on the deliverer, but on the *oppressor*. We are, in this chapter, seeing the story from the "other side." We are being forced to follow in the footsteps of the oppressing king and watch as he systematically tyrannizes over Israel.

We are being forced to follow in the footsteps of the oppressing king and watch as he systematically tyrannizes over Israel.

This switch of perspective is easy for the narrator because, in this story, a major change has occurred: the oppressor is himself an Israelite. We no longer have a foreign king and a foreign country invading and ransacking the nation. No longer do we have Syrians led by King Cushan-Rishataim, or Moabites with King Eglon, but rather the Israelites of Shechem led by King Abimelech, who terrorizes the land of Israel for three years. The oppression of Israel has come home to roost. In the famous words of the comic strip Pogo, "We have met the enemy, and he is us!"

Since the story of Abimelech focuses mostly upon the oppression that he brings, practically the whole story relates to his tactics with little space given to his downfall and death. The story of Abimelech falls naturally into five parts. First, the story relates how Abimelech conspires with his relatives in Shechem to convince their political leaders to crown him as their ruler. After they agree to do this and give him money, he hires mercenaries ("worthless and reckless fellows"), goes to his father's hometown of Ophrah, and slaughters all seventy of his half-brothers "on a single stone." He returns to Shechem, where the city crowns Abimelech king.

At the mention of Abimelech's murder of his brothers and his coronation as king, we expect a deliverer to appear and bring vengeance upon Abimelech's head. And this seems to occur in the next section. Jotham, Abimelech's youngest brother from Ophrah, has escaped the slaughter and pronounces judgment against Abimelech and the leaders of Shechem. He tells a parable about the trees, which hints that only unscrupulous people seek political power. He then pronounces a long indictment against Abimelech. But, at the end of his speech, instead of rising against his half-brother and bringing deliverance, he runs away because he, like his father Gideon before him, is afraid of confronting the oppressor.

In the next section another possible deliverer arises, this time a more unlikely candidate. A man named Gaal son of Ebed (which means "loathsome son of a slave") moves into Shechem. Is he to be Israel's deliverer? The leaders of Shechem trust him and are willing to follow him as he rages against Abimelech, who is out of town. The ruler of the city, Zebul, however, hears Gaal's insults and warns Abimelech about the intended coup. Abimelech rounds up his troops and soundly beats the lords of Shechem and Zebul, and himself chases Gaal out of town.

Next, Abimelech's rage causes him to perpetrate further acts of violence. Unsatisfied with punishing the lords of Shechem, he turns and destroys most of the inhabitants of the town, tears the city down, and sows the ground with salt. The remaining inhabitants take refuge in the city's watchtower, which Abimelech and his troops burn; he kills about a thousand men and women. Next, he travels to a nearby city, Thebez, and wages war against it, in spite of the fact that they have done nothing against him. The inhabitants of Thebez take refuge in their watchtower and Abimelech attempts to burn that down as well.

The end of the story is quick and ironic—

> A certain woman threw an upper millstone on Abimelech's head, and crushed his skull. Immediately he called to the young man who carried his armor and said to him, "Draw your sword and kill me, so people will not say about me, 'A woman killed him.'" So the young man thrust him through, and he died (9:53–54).

In a wonderful parallel with the earlier story of Jael, a lone woman destroys the enemy of Israel within a single verse by fatally striking his head. Unlike Sisera, however, Abimelech cannot stand his fate of being killed by a woman and orders his armor-bearer to run him through, which he does. The irony, of course, is that the story does not allow Abimelech's lie to be the true tale. The reader knows the truth: a single nameless woman is the deliverer of Israel in the story. When Israel sees their oppressor dead, they return home and the cycle comes to an end.

The reader knows the truth: a single nameless woman is the deliverer of Israel in the story.

The story of Abimelech stands at the center of the book of Judges for a good reason. Up to this point, sin, oppression, and deliverance were three separate segments of the story cycle; the oppressor and the oppressed were two very different groups of people, and the stories have been about deliverance from a fate that Israel has deserved. But, because Israel persists in its unfaithfulness time and time and time again, the story has become quite complicated. The sin of Israel here leads to a time of oppression both of and by Israel. The oppressor and the oppressed are both Israelites, so now Israel itself is its own oppressor.

At its base, however, the story is still about God's deliverance of Israel from their domination. Earlier, during the incident of Jotham's escape from death, the narrator steps out of the perspective of King Abimelech and informs us of God's purpose:

> But God sent an evil spirit between Abimelech and the lords of Shechem; and the lords of Shechem dealt treacherously with Abimelech. This happened so that the violence done to the seventy sons of Jerubbaal might be avenged and their blood be laid on their brother Abimelech, who killed them, and on the lords of Shechem, who strengthened his hands to kill his brothers (9:23–24).

Here, God does not send the spirit upon a deliverer in order to strengthen him for winning a battle. Instead, the spirit here is "evil" and is sent against the oppressors themselves—Abimelech and his mercenaries. Furthermore, Israel's deliverance from oppression does not take the form of a military leader who wins a battle, but derives from the treachery and disloyalty of the oppressors themselves. And, to make perfectly clear that the story is just the same as the previous cycles, even though told from the perspective of the oppressor, the narrator assures us at the very end of the story,

> Thus God repaid Abimelech for the crime he committed against his father in killing his seventy brothers; and God also made all the wickedness of the people of Shechem fall back on their heads, and on them came the curse of Jotham son of Jerubbaal (9: 56–57).

The moral of this story could not be any clearer.

Minor Characters: Tola and Jair (Judges 10:1–4)

After the death of Abimelech, we expect from all that has gone before that Israel will fall into sin and the cycle will begin once more. But, instead, we have a short interlude and are introduced to two judges. The short notices of the judgeships of Tola and Jair not only interrupt the expected pattern, they do so in an interesting way.

If you remember, at the end of the story of Ehud, there appeared a similarly brief notice about Shamgar, which was interesting because it contained no mention of Israel's sin or subsequent oppression. Shamgar's story simply mentions his deliverance of Israel, with little else included. Here the stories of Tola and Jair also have no mention of sin or oppression—or deliverance, either. Neither one fights for or delivers Israel, but they simply "judge" Israel, in a way that resembles the work of Deborah before she commissions Barak to fight Israel's enemies. Here, however, Tola and Jair seem to be more like politicians or office-holders than warriors. In light of the increasing violence perpetrated both by Israel and upon Israel in the last chapter and in the chapters to come, their presence here is troubling. The only thing the narrator tells us about them is their hometowns and, in the case of Jair, how influential his thirty sons are. No mention about deliverance; no mention about moral leadership. While their country is collapsing around their ears, Tola and Jair seem to have very successful and long lives, but do little to help.

Jephthah, the Deal-Making Judge (Judges 11:1–12:7)

With the beginning of the story of Jephthah, it appears that we are back on track with the familiar pattern. Israel, we are told, again falls away from its worship of God, turning not merely to the Baals and Asherahs of earlier times, but to a multiplicity of gods—"the Baals and the Astartes, the gods of Aram, the gods of Sidon, the gods of Moab, the gods of the Ammonites, and the gods of the Philistines." In good order, God responds by giving Israel into the hand of oppressors, the Philistines and the Ammonites. Notice, however, that it is not into the hand of a particular king that Israel falls, as it had been before. The source of their oppression is more general; the entire countries of Philistia and Ammon are their oppressors. In order to free themselves, they now cannot simply kill the king; they must defeat the entire nation.

Again, as we would expect, Israel responds to their conquest by again crying out to God. But here the story begins to become complicated. God does not respond with mercy and raise up a deliverer to rescue the people. As had been mentioned in both of the introductions to the book, Israel seems to have brought itself to a state where mere deliverance from enemies will not help. Because of their constant habit of faithlessness, the cyclical pattern of sin, oppression, and deliverance no longer functions to train and discipline Israel to remain faithful. God acknowledges the fact that military deliverance would not offer true deliverance at all. He sees that the only way out of the situation is to let Israel remain under the authority of those whom they have freely chosen, the Philistines and Ammonites. When Israel persists in crying out for help, and when the pagan images

Because of their habit of faithlessness, the cyclical pattern of sin, oppression, and deliverance no longer functions to train and discipline Israel to remain true.

of the foreign gods are removed, God mercifully relents. (Whether, however, this is truly an instance of mercy is yet to be seen.) The leaders of the Israelite region of Gilead agree to appoint someone over them who will be their head, who will "begin to fight" against the Ammonites. We, like the inhabitants of Gilead, naturally begin to wonder. Who might this deliverer be?

The introduction of Jephthah should sound very familiar. He is born of a woman who is not the wife of his father—in this case, a prostitute. His half-brothers, who despise him, drive him away to live in the land of Tob. Jephthah, in response to being cast out, gathers renegades and outlaws around him, who go out raiding the neighboring area. The family structure and Jephthah's response to it sound almost identical to Abimelech's in the previous chapter. Based upon the parallel, we might expect Jephthah to go and kill off his family as Abimelech did. In this case, however, it is the brothers who seek reconciliation with Jephthah, asking him to be their head and to fight against the Ammonites for them. Although at this point we may suspect that he is the hoped-for deliverer, Jephthah does not immediately seize the opportunity and go out and fight against the Ammonites. Instead he attempts to make a deal with his half-brothers: "If you bring me home again to fight with the Ammonites, and the LORD gives them over to me, I will be your head" (11:9). Jephthah tries to take control of the situation not through direct action, but through deal-making. He uses his speech to try to get what he wants out of the situation.

The Gileadites bring him back, and make him their head. According to the agreement, Jephthah should at this point go to war against the Ammonites. But, no, he remains in Gilead and does what he does best: he tries to make a deal with the enemy. He begins the negotiations by asking why the Ammonites have attacked the region of Gilead. The king of Gilead explains that it is a matter of justice, for Israel had stolen the land from Ammon during their flight from Egypt. This is a significant change in the pattern; by engaging the Ammonites in this way, Jephthah has shifted the focus. No longer are the Israelites' sufferings at the hand of the Ammonites a punishment for breaking the covenant with God and worshiping pagan gods, but merely a matter of historical and political realities. Suddenly the reason for the Ammonites' attack on Gilead is not to be found in God's anger at Israel's disloyalty, but in past grievances between Israel and Ammon.

Jephthah responds to the Ammonite king with a defense. In the longest single speech in the book of Judges, Jephthah recounts the events that are found, more or less, in Numbers 20–24, detailing the encounters of Israel with the kings of the Edomites, the Amorites, the Moabites, and the inhabitants of Bashan. Jephthah argues that Israel never encroached on Ammonite land in the past, and the land that Israel did take was won by them legally through defensive warfare. In arguing in this way, however, Jephthah completely circumvents the theological reason why Ammon has been oppressing them, which is Israel's apostasy. Thus instead of simply mustering his troops and fighting off the Ammonites, he tries to argue his way out of the situation, with the result that the Ammonite king ignores him. The longest speech in the book of Judges has absolutely no effect whatsoever. All of the negotiations are completely worthless and lead nowhere, neither to the deliverance of Israel or to a deepening of Israel's faithfulness toward God.

Finally, the spirit of the LORD comes upon Jephthah and he heads to Ammon. We expect the battle to be fought and won rather quickly. But Jephthah has one more piece of negotiation to try, and that is to make a deal with God. If God will give the Ammonites into his hand, then Jephthah will, in turn, make a sacrifice to God when he returns home. Exactly what Jephthah will sacrifice is left up to chance. In English it sounds a bit shocking: "Whoever comes out of the doors of my house to meet me . . . shall be the LORD's, to be offered up by me as a burnt offering." In Hebrew it reads a bit more ambiguously, as "that which comes out of my house. . . ." In the architectural style of the time, the barn was on the bottom floor of the house and the human occupants lived on the second floor and the roof, so Jephthah undoubtedly expected to encounter a sheep or a goat that he would sacrifice. But why make the deal with God at all? I believe it is because that is what Jephthah does. He makes deals.

"Whoever comes out of the doors of my house to meet me . . . shall be the LORD's, to be offered up by me as a burnt offering."

After making his vow, once the battle begins it is won rather quickly and, seemingly, easily. The entire defeat of the Ammonites is told in exactly two verses. Having won the war and delivered Israel, we expect the next sentence to tell us that the land had rest for the remainder of Jephthah's life and that he died at a certain advanced age. But it is not to be. The stories from Gideon onward describe the period of deliverance to be as troubling as the time of oppression. And here, Jephthah—true to form—fulfills this pattern.

For upon coming to his home, it is not a sheep or a calf that he sees first, but his daughter, his only child. When he sees her, he acknowledges his grief but then blames her for troubling him:

> When he saw her, he tore his clothes, and said, "Alas, my daughter! You have brought me very low; you have become the cause of great trouble to me. For I have opened my mouth to the Lord, and I cannot take back my vow" (11: 35).

Jephthah does not see his vow to be the problem, nor his tendency to make deals, but his own daughter. And what is his response? Does he, at this troubling and morally uncertain time, attempt to renegotiate the vow? Or does he simply interpret the vow in the way that it was undoubtedly intended, and take the next sheep or calf that comes out of the door as a sacrifice? No, for the first time in the story, Jephthah does not negotiate. He intends to fulfill his vow. So the daughter of Jephthah, herself, is reduced to having to negotiate with her father. She asks for two months of respite so that she and her friends may go and mourn the fact that she will die without having had children. He grants her wish, but at the end of the period, he "did to her according to the vow he had made." It is as if the narrator cannot even straightforwardly report Jephthah's slaughter of his own daughter; it is too horrendous to tell.

Jephthah's inclination to violence, however, does not end there. In a scene that parallels an incident in the story of Gideon, the Ephraimites come to Jephthah and complain that they were not called to fight against the Ammonites. Their rage causes them to follow up on their question with a threat: "We will burn your house down over you!" But where Gideon assuaged the Ephraimites' anger by praising them, Jephthah does no such thing for his fellow Israelites. Asserting that he did call them but they did not come, he then musters his troops and wages a full-scale war against Ephraim, slaughtering forty-two Ephraimites on the battlefield.

It seems that with his enemies and with God, negotiation and dealmaking is how Jepthah does business, but with his own family or with his fellow Israelites, he no longer negotiates but slaughters and wages total war upon any who trouble him. It is no surprise, then, that the story of Jephthah ends with his death and burial, but the regular and comforting sentence, "The land had rest in the days of Jephthah," is not found here. It seems as if life, for Israel, has become as violent and as deathly in their period of deliverance as it was in their period of oppression. There is little difference here. The only question that remains as we look back over the cycle is: who does the oppressing in this story, the Ammonites or Israel's deliverer, Jephthah?

At the end of the Jephthah story, the violence once reserved for foreign oppressors is now turned against an innocent young women and fellow Israelites. We might hope for someone to come along and bring the "rest" that is so lacking for Israel. Instead, we meet in Judges 12 three "minor judges" who are similar to Tola and Jair earlier. As before, these judges seem to do little. They have large families, which seems to assure them of some sort of stability, but we know nothing besides the fact that they judged Israel for seven, ten, and eight years respectively. There are no stories of rescue and deliverance. It may be that these judges, as well as Tola and Jair, have been added to the sequence in order to bring the number up to twelve. This would fulfill a pattern, with a different judge from each of the twelve tribes of Israel. This certainly may be so and I do not doubt it. But I wonder about these "minor judges." Why does Shamgar, who heroically battles against the Philistines, appear in the first half of the book, while Tola, Jair, Ibzan, Elon, and Abdon, whose only virtues seem to be their large families and quantities of livestock, appear near the end of the series of judge stories? Perhaps the former warriors and leaders of Israel have become, here at the end of the series, bureaucrats at best, maintaining the status quo, and at their worst have themselves become the oppressors of Israel. There is, however, one more judge in the series. Perhaps it will be he who will finally deliver Israel and lead the Israelites to repentance and faithfulness.

Perhaps the former warriors and leaders of Israel have become bureaucrats, keeping the status quo, and at their worst becoming the oppressors of Israel.

Samson, the Anti-Judge (Judges 13:1–16:31)

From one perspective, the stories of Samson are the best in the book of Judges. They also make up the longest of the cycles, covering five long chapters and following him from his conception and birth all the way to his death. The stories focused on Samson are also some of the funniest in the entire Bible. Sexual innuendo and wordplay (at least in the Hebrew version) are woven into almost every scene. It is no surprise, therefore, that if you are familiar with anything at all about the book of Judges, you will probably know the stories about Samson.

In light of the book as a whole, however, and considering what the book is about, the stories of Samson are extremely frustrating. We can see the exasperating nature of the stories from the very first verse of the cycle. It begins in the usual way:

> The Israelites again did what was evil in the sight of the LORD, and the LORD gave them into the hand of the Philistines forty years (13:1).

The previous statements about the sin of Israel have also recorded the length of their oppression: eight years under King Cushan-Rishataim, eighteen years under King Eglon, twenty years under King Jabin, seven years under the Midianites, eighteen years under the Ammonites. Yet this latest oppression lasts twice as long as any previous period. While it is true that part of the reason for the length is that the deliverer, Samson, must first be born and grow up, it is also true that even when he becomes a man, he will do little to deliver Israel from the Philistines. He will look less like an Israelite leader and more like a Philistine

The stories of Samson are some of the funniest in the entire Bible, with sexual innuendo and wordplay woven into almost every scene.

prankster. If Samson is truly a deliverer of Israel, we must wait a long, long time to see him do what must be done.

Except for the initial notice about Israel doing "what was evil in the sight of the LORD," and the notice of their being given into the hand of the Philistines, along with the summary statement at the end that Samson had judged Israel for twenty years, the usual pattern of the judge stories is missing. There is no extended example of how the Philistines oppress Israel, for example, and no scene of Israel crying out in their trouble. Nor is there any explicit statement of how God "raised up" Samson or of God delivering the Philistines into his hand, or of a complete victory over them. In short, the cycle, except for the very beginning and the very end, is completely missing. What takes its place are a series of extended scenes focused solely upon Samson's prank-filled life.

The one motif from previous judge stories that does appear several times in the Samson cycle is the theme of the "spirit of the LORD" rushing upon him. In the previous stories, this appearance of the spirit signals either outright deliverance of Israel, as with Othniel, or the judge's preparation for the decisive battle, as with Gideon. Although the spirit impels or "rushes" upon Samson on four separate occasions, in none of them does he win any decisive victory over the Philistines. In one case, we are simply told that the spirit "begins to stir" him when he reaches maturity, but nothing comes of it. In another case, the spirit's presence causes him to kill a young lion who roars at him, but nothing more comes of it. In the third case, the presence of the spirit allows him to kill thirty Philistines in order to take their clothing as a payment for a foolish wager he had made, but nothing else. In the final scene, the spirit rushing upon him empowers Samson to break the ropes with which he has been bound and to kill one thousand Philistines with a donkey's jawbone. While this may seem impressive at first sight, we soon learn that this also did little to win deliverance for Israel against the Philistines. So even the use of a major motif from earlier stories merely reveals that Samson is ultimately insignificant in bringing about any sort of liberation for Israel.

The Samson cycle falls into four general stories, which roughly correspond with its four chapters. In chapter 13, we are told about his conception and birth. Samson's parents are from the tribe of Dan. The angel of the LORD meets his mother and foretells his birth— her child would be a Nazirite, dedicated to the worship of God even from the womb. According to Numbers 6, the Nazirites were forbidden to drink any sort of alcohol, to come in contact with any corpse, or to shave the hair of their head. These three constraints signified their special relationship with God.

> According to Numbers 6, the Nazirites were forbidden to drink any sort of alcohol, to come in contact with a corpse, or to shave the hair of their head.

In connection with the announcement of Samson's birth, his father Manoah appears to be rather dim-witted (which may be where Samson gets it from). Even though his wife tells him exactly what the child and she must to do to fulfill the vow placed upon them, Manoah does not seem to believe her or to understand the (rather simple and straightforward) instructions. When he has the chance to meet the angel of the LORD afterwards, he asks "What is to be the boy's rule of life; what is he to do?" The angel directs Manoah's attention, again, to his wife, who has perfectly understood the situation. Manoah presses the angel to eat, which he refuses to do, and to reveal his name, which he also refuses. Once Manoah presents his meal and it miraculously is consumed in a flame and the angel ascends into heaven, Manoah supposes that he and his wife will die, which they will not. Manoah, time and time again, does not understand what is going on in his surroundings. He does, however, ask an important question about his expected son: "What is he to do?" That is a question that we must not lose sight of in the following stories. What is Samson supposed to be doing?

The story of Samson's birth ends with the spirit beginning to stir him in Mahaneh-dan (or, "the encampment of Dan"). We might expect that this activity of the spirit will lead him to win the victory over the Philistines, but if so we will be sorely disappointed.

In chapter 14, Samson wants to marry a Philistine woman he sees in Timnah. Although his father tries to dissuade him, Samson remains stalwart; he wants his father to get her for him. Verse 4 provides one of the few theological insights of the cycle: "His father and mother did not know that this was from the LORD; for he was seeking a pretext to act against the Philistines. At that time the Philistines had dominion over Israel." In English, this sounds a bit like God was trying to find a reason to defeat the Philistines; he was seeking a "pretext." In fact, the reason why God wants to defeat the Philistines is found in the next sentence: they have dominion over Israel. God isn't seeking a pretext to defeat Philistia, he is, rather, seeking "an opportunity" (Hebrew *to'anah*) to act against the Philistines. In light of the activity of God so far in the book, this is remarkable. Israel, through her continuous faithlessness, has finally so enmeshed itself in an oppressive situation that God must actively "seek an opportunity to act." No longer can the simple rushing of the spirit or the raising up of a deliverer suffice. God is reduced to having to scheme and plan and look for various ways to work.

On his journey down to Timnah, Samson kills a lion and scrapes honey from the carcass and eats it, and then gives the honey to his parents who also eat it. This act signifies that the Nazirite vow about not touching a corpse is broken; Samson takes the first step toward his own faithlessness and destruction almost before he begins. Once in Timnah, Samson makes a feast (Hebrew *mishteh*, or "drinking party") for those attending his wedding. The implication is clear: the second of his Nazirite vows, which forbids alcohol, is now broken as well.

Eating honey from the lion's carcass breaks the first of Samson's Nazirite vows, which is never to touch a corpse.

Samson consistently sees himself as smart, wily, and more insightful than others. He therefore puts a riddle to his future Philistine family, a riddle that is not based on wordplay or innuendo but on a secret that only he knows. When his relatives cannot answer the riddle, they threaten Samson's future wife and her family with violence, just as the Ephraimites threatened Jephthah. She eventually coaxes the secret from Samson and, by using the spirit's power for his own purposes, he pays his wager by killing thirty Philistines in Ashkelon.

As a result of his disastrous pre-wedding party, Samson's wife is given to his best man. When Samson hears of it he threatens, "This time, when I do mischief to the Philistines, I will be without blame." His threat, however, does not lead him to muster Israelite troops and defeat the Philistines, but rather to catch foxes and send them, with torches tied to their tails, through the wheat fields, the olive groves, and the vineyards of the Philistines. This only causes the Philistines to carry out their earlier threat: they burn Samson's fiancée and her family. Samson takes vengeance on the Philistines by fighting them in a "great slaughter," but one that does not win Israel's freedom. When he is handed over to the Philistines by Ephraim, he picks up a donkey's jawbone and kills one thousand of them.

Although we are told that Samson "judged Israel in the days of the Philistines twenty years," it is not during a period of freedom and autonomy. Israel is still under the domination of a foreign power. What, in this context, can "judging Israel" possibly mean? It seems as if Israel's oppression and its freedom, the time spent under a foreign power and the time spent under a homegrown judge, are all the same by this point. Words such as "oppression" and "deliverance" have lost all meaning.

Samson's story ends with the relationships he has with two women and their aftermath, one a prostitute in Gaza and the other a woman named Delilah from the valley of Sorek. In the former story, Samson lies with a prostitute in Gaza and when the inhabitants find out that Samson is in their city, they surround the city gate all night, hoping to catch him as he leaves the gates in the morning. Samson, however, arises at midnight, grasps the city gates and carries them to the top of a hill. This is quite a trick, but does little to rescue Israel from their oppressors.

Next, he falls in love with Delilah. She is bribed by the lords of the Philistines to make Samson reveal the secret of his strength. When first questioned, he lies and says that fresh bowstrings will make him weak; when she binds him, he breaks them like thread. When questioned again, he tells her that new ropes will incapacitate him, again to no avail. Next he tells Delilah that if she weaves his hair on a loom, then this strength would leave him; after she does so, he destroys the loom and all the weavings that are upon it.

Three times she has done exactly what he has said. When, however, she continues to pester him, Samson falls apart like a child and tells the truth—if he were shaved, that would negate his vow and he would become like any human being. It should come as no surprise, either to the reader or to Samson himself, that Delilah does exactly what he has said. She hires a barber and, as Samson sleeps, she has

him shave his hair. Just like Jael and Sisera earlier, Delilah here sub-
dues her people's enemy by putting him to sleep and doing something to his head:

> He began to weaken, and his strength left him. Then she said, "The
> Philistines are upon you, Samson!" When he awoke from his sleep, he
> thought, "I will go out as at other times, and shake myself free." But he
> did not know that the Lord had left him. So the Philistines seized him
> and gouged out his eyes. They brought him down to Gaza and bound
> him with bronze shackles; and he ground at the mill in the prison
> (16:19–21).

Yet again we have stepped through the looking glass. It is no longer
an ally of Israel who defeats the foreign oppressor, but the foreigner
who defeats the Israelite deliverer. Samson has become the anti-hero.
The story is one of complete victory, but the vic-
tory has been won by the oppressors of Israel.

*It is no longer an ally of Israel
who defeats the foreign
oppressor, but the foreigner
who defeats the Israelite.*

In the final scene of the cycle, we have fully
reached the inverse of where we began so many
chapters before. The leaders of the Philistines
gather and sacrifice to their god Dagon because, in
their words, "Our god has given Samson our enemy into our hand."
Their sacrifice causes the general population of the Philistines to
join in their worship, because "the ravager of our country, who was
killed many of us" has been defeated. How ironic! How similar are
these Philistines to the Israelites after the victories of Othniel, Ehud,
and Deborah—God has miraculously delivered their enemy into
their hands and their response is faithful worship. Here, near the end
of the cycle, Samson's defeat also inspires heartfelt worship on the
part of the victor, but the victor is not Israel.

Samson dies as he lived, with the Philistines. In this final act, he is
brought out to entertain the Philistines who have gathered to rejoice
over their victory. The last of the judges is brought out to do what he
does best, which is to make people laugh. And, with his last bit of
strength, he topples the central two columns in the hall and kills the
Philistines who were attending the celebration as well as himself.
What is the final assessment? "Those he killed at his death were more

than those he had killed during his life" (v. 30). In light of the oppression of Israel and in light of what "the boy was supposed to do," this should not be seen as praise, but as a negative judgment. Samson routs and kills many Philistines, but he never wins a decisive victory, never frees Israel from bondage. Throughout his time as a judge Israel is under foreign rule; he lives like a Philistine and dies with the Philistines. At the end of the day Samson is able to do two things well: he can entertain and he can inspire people to worship foreign gods. If this is what "deliverance" and "salvation" and "judgeship" has come to, it is quite clear that something else must be done. The cyclical pattern of the previous fourteen chapters finally dies out not with a bang, but a whimper.

CHAPTER FIVE

Things Fall Apart:
The Conclusions

Many people encounter the Bible in the same way they would watch an old-time western. They read a particular story or book and ask two primary questions: "What's going on in the story?" and "Who are good guys and who are the bad guys?" The first question is, of course, perfectly natural and important. We cannot understand what a story may be about without understanding the basic plot, the simple storyline. In a very real sense, westerns (and movies in general) and biblical stories have this in common: The medium is the message. The story is the same "stuff" as its message. You cannot have one without the other.

The second question is more of a problem. Unlike traditional westerns, biblical stories rarely have purely "good characters" and "bad characters" in them. It is usually difficult deciding who wears the white hat or the black hat in biblical stories, whose characters are often a lot more like real human beings, like you and me. Even if a particular individual is a main character, this doesn't necessarily mean he or she is set up as a role model for the reader to follow. And even those characters who are clearly set up as "villains" often have traits and characteristics that we all can identify with and learn from. Biblical characters in stories often serve us best when they function like mirrors, giving us the chance to look at them and see ourselves in them—the good parts and bad parts of ourselves together. This insight is particularly important when interpreting a tragedy such as we find in the book of Judges. All the characters are important, and not because they are either "good guys" or "bad guys."

Reading biblical stories, for me, is a lot like watching the famous western *High Noon*. The storyline is relatively simple, but the characters are very complex. Will Kane, played by Gary Cooper, has been the longtime marshal of Hadleyville. At the beginning of the movie, he has just married a pacifist Quaker named Amy, played by Grace Kelly, turned in his badge, and is preparing to move away to become a storekeeper. Soon after the wedding, the town learns that Frank Miller, a ruthless criminal that Kane had brought to justice, is due to arrive on the noon train. Miller had been sentenced to the gallows, but was pardoned and released from jail. In court, he had vowed to take revenge on Kane and to kill anyone who got in his way. His three gang members wait for him at the station. The worried townspeople encourage Kane to leave, hoping to defuse the situation, but Kane has a crisis of conscience and turns back. He reclaims his badge and tries to gather others to help him, but it becomes clear that no one is willing to get involved. His deputy resigns. Only his former lover, Helen Ramírez, supports him, but there is little she can do to help. Kane's new wife threatens to leave on the noon train with or without him, but he stubbornly refuses to give in.

In the end, Kane faces the four gunmen alone. He guns down two of Miller's men, though he himself is wounded. Helen Ramírez and Amy both board the train, but Amy gets off when she hears the sound of gunfire. Choosing to fight and save her husband's life instead of holding to her religious beliefs, she kills the third gunman by shooting him in the back. Miller then takes her hostage and offers to trade her for Kane, who agrees, coming out into the open. Amy, however, takes Miller by surprise, clawing him in the face and forcing him to release her. Kane shoots and kills him. Then, as the townspeople emerge, he contemptuously throws his marshal's star in the dirt and leaves town with his wife. This is how the movie ends.

Although Will Kane is clearly the main character of *High Noon*, his motives are not as clear-cut as may appear. Does he stay to face Frank Miller out of a sense of duty? Out of a sense of self-preservation? Out of a sense of revenge? And what about the townspeople? Are they acting out of cowardice, or self-preservation, or their own sense of justice? Even though Kane "wins" his fight, he tosses his marshal's badge on the ground at the end of the movie, showing that victory isn't as simple or as "victorious" as we may think. The movie provides us a way of thinking about our own sense of justice, about what such ideas really mean in our own very complex lives. In *High Noon*, while there are "bad guys," there aren't any purely "good guys." Human nature is too complex. As Solzhenitsyn wrote in *The Gulag Archipelago*, "The line dividing good and evil cuts through the heart of every human being. And who is willing to destroy a piece of his own heart?"[13] This is what we are also finding with most of the characters in the book of Judges— and here, near the end of the book, the characters are complex indeed.

Thus far in the book of Judges, we have met numerous deliverers of Israel. One of them, Othniel, has been portrayed as the best. The rest—Ehud, Deborah and Barak, Jael, Gideon, Jephthah, and Samson—have been progressively less admirable while still playing the part of the liberators of Israel from their oppression. We have also met other characters like Shamgar, the deliverer without a story, Abimelech the evil king, and the "minor judges" Tola, Jair, Ibzan, Elon, and Abdon. Behind and throughout all of these stories, however, Israel itself has been shown to be increasingly unfaithful to God, turning their backs on the covenant and worshipping the Canaanite gods whenever they get a chance.

This moral slide toward irrelevance by the series of judge/ deliverers and by Israel itself has been accomplished both by their own individual failings as well by the continued disintegration of the normative pattern of sin, deliverance, peace, and renewed sin that we've seen over and over thus far. Here, near the end of the book, the center cannot hold. The pattern completely unravels.

Israel's moral slide toward irrelevance goes hand in hand with the disintegration of the pattern of sin, deliverance, peace, and renewed sin.

What Lies Behind the Two Conclusions

The ending of the book of Judges consists of two stories that are clearly different from anything that comes before. In these two concluding tales, we have no deliverers and no judges, nor do we have the accustomed pattern of sin, oppression, deliverance, and rest that we have seen over and over since its inauguration in the second introduction. None of these themes explicitly appear either by means of the usual formulas ("Now Israel did what was evil in the sight of the LORD" or "So God raised up for them a deliverer") or even by hints and allusions. These stories, it has been assumed, are clearly "doing something else" than those about Ehud, Gideon, or Samson.

This difference has led many scholars to believe that the concluding stories must have come from the hand of another editor, and not those who first organized the central stories. The assumption behind this, however, seems to be that books, or on a smaller scale stories, must only do one thing in one way. If there is a different or unexpected theme or pattern or theological perspective, so this thinking goes, it must have been added on by a different author.

> In those days there was no king in Israel; all the people did what was right in their own eyes (17:6).

I would argue that although the usual pattern of sin, oppression, deliverance, and rest is not found here at the end of the book, the two conclusions of the book do have their own constant refrain. Near their beginning, scattered twice within, and at their end is a notice about the absence of a king in, or over, Israel:

> In those days there was no king in Israel; all the people did what was right in their own eyes (17:6).

> In those days there was no king in Israel (18:1).

> In those days, when there was no king in Israel ... (19:1).

> In those days there was no king in Israel; all the people did what was right in their own eyes (21:25).

This four-fold refrain is usually interpreted as coming from the person or persons who "added" the conclusions to the end of the tales of the judges. The two epilogues, according to this view, were probably added when the Deuteronomistic History as a whole was brought together and organized. This much, I believe, is a possible and even probable explanation of the epilogues.

What of the four-fold refrain? What does it mean? Most scholars think that the remark about there being "no king in Israel" looks forward to the next book in the History, 1 Samuel, and the rise of the kingship in Israel at that time. Thus the chaos found in the concluding stories is meant to introduce the theological rationale for the monarchy found in the next book. These final chapters, therefore, function more like an introduction to 1 Samuel and less like a conclusion to the book of Judges. At least that seems to be the scholarly consensus.

For my part, I do not think that the concluding stories have to be interpreted this way. I think they can be interpreted as part of the book of Judges and as fitting conclusions to the long, increasingly desperate story that we have seen thus far. It is true, very often, that parts of books that have little to do with their surrounding subject might come from another hand. When a pattern that is found throughout a book unexpectedly disappears from the plot, this often is an indication that something else is going on. But this is not what we actually do find in Judges as a whole. The disappearance of the pattern that formerly characterized the stories of the earlier judges in the main part of the book is an appropriate ending for this story.

No, we do not see warrior-deliverers in the stories; this is quite in line with the trajectory taken by the book as a whole. The judges have become less and less able to deliver Israel from its enemies, mostly because the character of Israel itself becomes its own worst enemy. Nor do we see the regular pattern in the conclusions as we saw in the deliverance stories; but this is, also, quite understandable. The pattern has consistently and continuously become fainter and fainter as the chaos both within Israel and within its leaders has increased. We should not be surprised to see that pattern disappear completely by the end of the book.

The worsening character of Israel itself is its own worst enemy.

Finally, the regular refrain of "In those days there was no king in Israel" need not only be seen as a forward-looking, hopeful sentiment for better days ahead once the Israelite monarchy has been established. It can also be seen in light of the book as a whole. The linchpin for the four-fold cycle is the coming of the oppressor. The coming of each oppressor is the result of Israel's sin; it is the oppressor that makes deliverance necessary. And it is the time of Israel's subjugation that serves as the counterpart to "and the land had rest." If the oppressor—if the "king"—were to be removed from any cycle, all would be lost. Israel would find itself mired in its faithlessness, ignorantly and blindly doing whatever it thought best.

Therefore, without the presence of Cushan-Rishataim, Eglon, Jabin and Sisera, Zebah and Zalmunna, without Abimelech himself, or the Ammonites and the Philistines—in short, if there were no enemies in Judges, there could be no "judge cycle" in the book. Without a king over Israel, oppressing Israel and in a sense waking Israel up from its faithless lethargy, the Israelites would simply continue in their violent and apostate existence. In other words, if there were "no king over Israel," everyone would simply do whatever was right in their own eyes. And this is precisely what we have at the end of the tragedy of the book of Judges.

First Conclusion: Micah's Apostasy and the Destruction of Laish (Judges 17–18)

The first conclusion is composed of three interconnected stories: the family of Micah and the setting up of an illicit shrine in his home, Micah's hiring of a young Levite to be the priest of his shrine, and the tribe of Dan destroying the city of Laish. Interspersed between these three stories is the refrain, "In those days there was no king in Israel" (17:6a; 18:1a). The first of these also includes the ominous second statement: "All the people did what was right in their own eyes" (17:6b). These statements organize the three stories and provide the thematic "center" for them. The center, however, is a statement about what is *not* there, what is missing.

We come into the first conclusion in the middle of the action, where Micah is speaking to his mother about events that had occurred in the past. She had been the victim of a theft, losing eleven hundred pieces of silver, she had uttered a curse (either on the silver itself or upon the thief), and she had spoken that curse when Micah was listening. Micah also reveals two other pieces of information to his mother. The first is that he has the silver. This could be interpreted by the mother in several different ways. Perhaps the son found the silver somewhere, abandoned by the thief. Perhaps Micah apprehended the thief himself, and retrieved the money. Or, third, perhaps Micah was himself the thief. His second statement clears up the ambiguity: "I took it." He confesses that he was the thief and that he will return the stolen money to his mother.[14] His mother joyfully (and surprisingly) responds with a blessing: "May my son be blessed by the LORD." So far, in two short verses, we have a story of sin and forgiveness, cursing turned into blessing. Unfortunately (as we have seen throughout Judges), things quickly fall from this state of reconciliation to utter chaos.

Upon receiving the silver back, Micah's mother expresses her intention to use it as a gift for her repentant son. She plans to make it into a cast idol, which she does, and it stays in Micah's house. Then Micah, develops an entire mini-temple, complete with the shrine, vestments (the "ephod"), supporting idols (the "teraphim"), and one of his own sons as its priest. In a scene reminiscent of the end of the Gideon story, Micah dabbles in the illicit worship of both the LORD and of other gods. And, as with Gideon's cultic site, we expect the shrine to become a snare for both Micah's family and all Israel, leading to their downfall.

But unlike the Gideon story, we do not have the subsequent rise of an evil king to drive Israel back to God. The narrator notes that, in spite of these actions, no king appears in Israel. There is no Abimelech to punish. There is no king to discipline. As opposed to the cycle throughout Judges, there is no statement that these people are doing "what is evil in the sight of the LORD." Rather, Micah, his mother, his son—all of them continue to do whatever is "right in their own eyes." Everyone in the story is able to do what they wish. Israel is not under the heavy hand of a foreign power nor does it serve a tyrannical king.

But this does not mean that Israel is not oppressed. In this story and throughout these conclusions, Israel's fall into servitude will not be brought about by a foreign nation nor by an Israelite; it will not even arise from Israel as a whole. Instead the oppression that we see in these final epilogues is part of every scene, is bound up within every action of each character. The intermeshing of these characters will weave a web of oppression that becomes as insidious as it becomes intractable. Israel has become the source of its own captivity as well as the oppressed character. And in such a situation deliverance is not possible, for who can be the deliverer? And what would deliverance entail? Doing right? Not doing evil? But Israel has come to a point where even deciding what those words mean, and the difference between them, are impossible to distinguish. Everything that Israel will do from this point forward is always "right in their own eyes."

Israel's fall into servitude will not be brought about by a foreign nation or by any individual Israelite, but by Israel itself, trapped in a web of oppression.

The next story centers on the travels of a young man from Bethlehem who leaves his hometown and comes to Micah's house. Upon learning that the young man is a Levite and therefore able to perform priestly functions, Micah attempts to persuade him to stay and work for him as a priest within his newly formed shrine. He offers him pieces of silver, changes of clothes, and other incidentals. The Levite agrees to stay and do the priestly duties at the shrine, becoming "like one of his sons." Micah's response is telling. He assumes that, with a Levite—a person of an official priestly caste—working for him that "the LORD will prosper me" (v. 13). In other words Micah believes that he has, quite literally, bought the blessing of God.

And again we expect God to respond in some sort of way to limit or cut off these illicit actions. But, again, we are told that there is no response. No king arises. The individuals continue on their way.

At the close of this first conclusion, the entire tribe of Dan is searching for a place to live, much like the Levite in the previous scene. In a parallel to the famous story of the sending out of the spies in chapters 2 and 6 of the book of Joshua, the Danites also send spies into the land to seek out a place for the tribe to settle. As in the Joshua story, these spies also happen upon someone who assures them of their success, eventually conquering a city and resettling it for themselves. But here the similarities end. Whereas the story in Joshua affirmed divine protection for Israel and the miraculous destruction of the city of Jericho, complete with tumbling-down walls, the story of the tribe of Dan's migration illustrates their own cowardice and opportunism. It is also marked by the complete absence of any direct action on the part of God.

When the spies come to Micah's house, they find the young Levite and ask him what he was doing there. Whereas earlier, the narrator told us that Micah had "installed the Levite, and the young man became his priest" (17:12), the Levite tells the Danite spies his own perspective on the situation: "Micah ... hired me, and I have become his priest" (18:4). For the young Levite it isn't about a divine calling or about a priestly status. Priesthood for him is about being paid, what he can get out of his position. When the Danites further ask about their own mission, he assures them of God's protection: "The mission you are on is under the eye of the LORD" (v. 6).

When the Danites return to their tribe, they report that the land is good and that they can conquer an "unsuspecting people." As opposed to the earlier spy story in Joshua, where the city of Jericho is described in terms of strength and impregnability, the spies here seek the destruction of a defenseless city, one easily taken. As they lead the tribe and its army on the march, they come, again, to Micah's house and take advantage of the situation by removing his shrine and taking it with them, including the silver idol, the ephod, and the teraphim. When the Levite asks what they are doing, they make him an offer to become the priest to their entire tribe. Seeing a potentially lucrative opportunity, he himself gathers up the idol, ephod, and teraphim and leaves with them. When Micah chases after them and demands that they return his religious items, the Danites threaten him with death. He returns home empty-handed.

The Danites, for their part, take not only someone else's shrine and priest, but also someone else's city. They come to Laish, "to a people quiet and unsuspecting," and destroy it completely. In an interesting turn of affairs, the Canaanite city is "quiet." The word in Hebrew here is the same unusual word that concludes many of the stories of deliverance in the first part of the book: "the land had rest/quietude/peace." Here, it is the Canaanite city that has "quiet" and has no one to deliver it from the ravages of the Israelite tribe of Dan. Even though on the surface it may seem to be a triumphant story for the Israelites, the narrator

The people of Laish, "a people quiet and unsuspecting," have no one to deliver them from the ravages of the tribe of Dan.

89

skillfully portrays the Canaanite city in sympathetic terms and the invading Danites, along with their new, opportunistic Levite, in negative terms.

As for the theology of this first epilogue to Judges, throughout the story several characters mention what God wants and what God will do: "May my son be blessed by the LORD" (17:2b); "Now I know that the LORD will prosper me, because the Levite has become my priest" (17:13); "Go in peace. The mission you are on is under the eye of the LORD" (18: 6); "God has indeed given [the land] into your hands" (18:10). Before this point, God obviously acts in the lives of characters, leading them and helping them accomplish remarkable things. We have been told about these remarkable acts and God's purposes behind them by the narrator who has been telling the story. But here, in this first conclusion to the book, we have characters who have—in a sense—taken on the narrator's role. Micah's mother, Micah himself, and the young Levite talk about God and what God wants and how God acts. But are these statements true?

Does God bless Micah for telling the truth about the silver? Does God bless Micah because he has a Levite as a priest for his shrine? Is the mission of the Danites under the watchful and protective eye of God? Has God given the Danites the land, including the unsuspecting town of Laish? Has God done any of these things? And if not, why do the characters say that God has?

Are their statements true? Or are they lying in order to gain the goodwill of other characters? Or do they actually believe that they are telling the truth, but are mistaken? How do we, the readers of Judges, know what God's opinion is about Micah or about these Danites and their journey? Are Micah and the Danites doing "what is evil in the sight of the LORD"? Or are they merely doing "what is right in their own eyes"? To be honest, we have no way of knowing one way or the other.

The theology of the book parallels the patterns that we have seen. Early on, the regular patterns that organized the stories were easy to discern: sin, oppression, deliverance, and peace all played their part. Sometimes these themes were clear, sometimes a bit muddled, but they were always present. In the stories of Othniel, Ehud, Deborah, and Gideon the patterns were, more or less, present. Similarly, the theology of these early judge stories was usually clear and straight-forward. God was helping Israel to live in faithful relationship with themselves and with himself. When Israel failed to live up to their possibilities and slipped into unfaithfulness, God worked to bring them, eventually, back to that faithfulness. The pattern and the theology were for the most part simple and straightforward.

As the pattern disintegrates in the stories of Abimelech and Jephthah and Samson, even so the theological message becomes more complex. What is the purpose of the story of Abimelech, from a theological perspective? The narrator must intrude twice to tell us that the plot illustrates how the deception and treachery of Abimelech comes back on his own head; it is not apparent from the story itself. With Jephthah and Samson, the pattern almost completely unravels even as the theology becomes murkier. Here we have heroes that are not very heroic, and deliverance that does not truly deliver. Here we have stories that break the pattern, and in which God rarely acts openly and straightforwardly.

In the first of the epilogues, this situation declines even further. The pattern has disappeared, along with any theological perspective on sin, oppression, deliverance, or peace. The theology that was once so simple and straightforward, here at the end has become complex and messy.

Second Conclusion: The Sin of Gibeah and the Devastation of Benjamin (Judges 19–21)

The final conclusion to the book of Judges is one of the most violent in the whole Bible. The story of the family spat between a Levite man and his concubine that eventually leads to the near destruction of the entire tribe of Benjamin is a horrific tale. In the words of the biblical scholar Phyllis Trible, this story is truly a "text of terror." Read on its own, apart from the chapters that precede it, the story seems to be written only for its shock value and its unrelenting seeming gratuitous violence.

> *The final conclusion to the book of Judges is one of the most violent in the whole Bible, truly a "text of terror."*

If we try to find the "Word of God" in this terrible tale, removed from its context, in my opinion we will be searching in vain. The landscape of this tale is too blighted; the plot is too hopeless. What can we do in this situation? Some interpreters remove the text from the realm of theology and simply interpret it as a historical tradition about an unfortunate time in Israel's history. Some see it as a bit of folklore that reveals a chaotic time that is resolved (slightly) by the monarchy instituted in 1 Samuel. Is this final conclusion incapable of teaching us, therefore, about God or ourselves or our relationships? In short, how can this story speak theologically even in spite of its bleakness and violent plot?

The answer, I think, is by seeing it in terms of everything that has come before. When it is seen as the final coda to the tragic story before it, this final conclusion truly is a fitting end to the long slide of Israel from quick and easy success to utter and miserable failure. Time and again, the scenes of this story parallel earlier scenes in the book; its phrases echo earlier phrases; its characters mirror earlier characters. But here, at the tragic end, the scenes and phrases and characters are drawn with stark, heightened lines. What was once a simple tale of sin, oppression, deliverance, and rest is transformed into an inexorable nightmare where every turn leads further down the path to destruction, and not only for the concubine herself, or for the inhabitants of Gibeah, or for the members of the tribe of Benjamin. By the end of the story, with Israel's own self-awareness fragmented, both its sense of justice and its sense of mercy alike lead to chaos. Through its own faithlessness and constant desire to perpetrate "what was evil in the eyes of the LORD," Israel finds itself with nowhere to turn, unable to redeem itself and left to its own devices and desires. By the end, for Israel what is "good in their own eyes" and what is "evil in the eyes of the LORD" have become the same thing.

The story begins with a family quarrel between a Levite man and his concubine that echoes the argument between Samson and Delilah in chapter 16. When she runs away, the Levite travels from Ephraim to his concubine's family in Bethlehem, which is the inverse of the trek previously made by Micah's young Levite from Bethlehem to the hill country of Ephraim. While there, he keeps being delayed through the comic interference of his father-in-law, which will lead, eventually, to disaster. On the fifth day, the father-in-law delays his departure so late that the Levite must turn aside to the Benjaminite town of Gibeah to spend the night.

The Levite and the young woman are welcomed into the home of an old man, who provides them with a meal and a place to spend the night. The hospitality of the old man in Gibeah, however, is balanced by a violent attack by the men of the city, who threaten to rape the visitor in an attempt to humiliate him. Like Jephthah, the Levite callously sacrifices someone close to him to secure his own safely and security—he throws his concubine out of the house into the mob. After being raped and abused all night, the woman finds her way back to the home of the old man. But instead of caring for her and protecting her, the Levite hauls her back to his home in Ephraim and (reminiscent of Jephthah) kills her, cutting her into twelve pieces and sending her throughout the land of Israel. The people of Israel gather, in shock at what they have experienced. The Levite tells this story: "They intended to kill me and they raped my concubine until she died." No mention of the intent to rape him; no mention of his own throwing her out; no mention of her being alive the next morning. His half-truth finds fertile soil in the hearts of the men of Israel. Without leading any sort of investigation or finding corroboration, the men of Israel jump to the conclusion that the Levite is telling the truth (even in spite of his brutal butchery of the woman). As was true for Adoni-Bezek in chapter 1 and for King Abimelech in chapter 9, the theme of vengeance—paying back wrong for

Israel finds itself with nowhere to turn, unable to redeem itself and left to its own devices and desires.

wrong—reaches its climax here. Before, however, such an act could be seen as poetic justice on the unrighteous deeds of someone who sought the destruction of innocent people; here, it looks like simple, hate-filled revenge. Israel turns against itself and wages war upon its own people.

Like Jephthah, the men of Israel attempt to negotiate with the people of Benjamin: if they but turn over the evil men of Gibeah, no other harm will come to the tribe. But Benjamin, like the men of Gibeah and even all Israel, will not listen. They muster their army to protect their land from those who come to oppress them.

In a chilling parallel with the series of battles in chapter 1, Israel inquires of God who should lead the offensive against the enemy, against Benjamin. And God replies, "Judah shall go up first," which are the same exact words spoken in the first and more optimistic chapter of the book. There the battle was easy, the victory of Israel assured, and the enemy clear. Here, the battle is grueling, the victory difficult to attain, and the enemy is the Israelites themselves. Twice Israel asks God whether they should proceed and twice God says to go forward. Twice Israel is defeated and thousands die in the process. The divine oracles that, beforehand, were the assurance of victory here have changed into words of judgment. If Israel is both the oppressed and the oppressor, then there is no way to freedom and faithfulness. Israel, throughout the previous book, has finally, here, put itself in a place of no escape.

The primary tactic that defeats the Benjaminites is similar to that used by the evil King Abimelech when he defeated the rebellion of Gaal, the son of Ebed, and destroyed the city of Shechem. By letting the enemy believe they have the upper hand, a ragtag band of soldiers draws out the enemy from their stronghold city. When they are in the open field, thousands of other soldiers, hiding in ambush, rise up, cut off any retreat back to the city, and destroy the enemy army. With the exception of six hundred refugees, the entire tribe of Benjamin is wiped out. And the remainder of Israel vows that they will not provide any of their women to be wives for the remaining Benjaminite men, thus assuring the eventual elimination of the tribe.

And then a remarkable thing occurs: the conquerors feel sorry for their near-obliteration of Benjamin. But at this point in the tragedy, we suspect that even their attempt to repair the situation will only muddle it further. They attempt to find a way to keep the tribe viable and a part of the tribal alliance. Like Jephthah, however, they have made a vow and they will not go against it, even if doing so would most naturally—and justly—solve their problem.

Then they devise a solution. If any city did not come out to fight against Benjamin (even though they now acknowledge it was not the right thing to do), then that city should be destroyed and any virgin women in the city should be handed over to the remnant of the Benjaminites for wives. In earlier scenes in the book, when a group did not come out to fight alongside Israel, they were ritually cursed and their fate handed over to God. But here, Israel takes matters into its own hands and brings about the destruction of their neighbors themselves. They wipe out the population of Jabesh-Gilead and kidnap the four hundred virgins in the town, in order to hand them over to the remaining Benjaminites.

When, however, it is revealed that the number of the virgins is insufficient, Israel must devise another plan to acquire more. They advise the Benjaminites to kidnap the young women from the town of Shiloh as they come to dance during a religious festival. If the fathers of the young women complain, moreover, then the Israelites will simply tell them, callously, that it is all for the best. Through having their daughters kidnapped, they can help Israel correct their error in nearly wiping out Benjamin, but will not necessarily bring a curse on themselves for giving their daughters to Benjamin.

Throughout this final conclusion to the book, women have been reduced to being mere pawns in a very violent and treacherous series of circumstances. Previously the women of Israel appear as strong, redemptive characters, taking the initiative in their relationships (Achsah), judging Israel and leading its leaders into battle (Deborah), striking the fatal blow to those who would oppress Israel (Jael and the unnamed woman at the Tower of Thebez), and dedicating themselves and their children in devotion to God (Samson's mother). Even in their roles in the Samson cycle, the Philistine women often take control of the situation to bring down those who, in the reverse of the classic scene, are intent on oppressing their own people.

But here, at the end of Judges, the role of women is reduced to those who are retrieved, thrown out, raped, abused, killed, mutilated, captured, kidnapped, and bartered. They have been reduced to passive, nameless, faceless objects. This diminishment does not indicate any sort of inherent hatred of women on the part of ancient Israel, however. Seen from the perspective of the book as a whole, the role that women play in the book is the role that the confederacy of Israel plays. All descend from strength to weakness, from initiative to passivity, from unity to fragmentation, from life to death. At the end of the tragedy,

The role that women play in Judges is like that of Israel itself—all descend from strength to weakness, from initiative to passivity, and from life to death.

95

it is not only the female characters that are raped and dismembered and abused by the Israelites. It is that central character of Israel itself.

Near the end of the story, an important sentence is inserted before the final scene that captures this sad state of affairs. After giving the virgin women of Jabesh-Gilead to the Benjaminite survivors, the narrator ironically notes, "The people had compassion on Benjamin because the LORD had made a breach in the tribes of Israel" (21:15). At the end of the day, the Israelites see themselves as trying to redeem something that the LORD had, mistakenly, perpetrated against them. In their eyes it is the LORD who nearly destroyed Benjamin—not the half-truth of the Levite, not the rushing to judgment by the Israelites, not the foolish oath about not intermarrying with the Benjaminites, nor the vicious, genocidal tactics of the Israelite army. No, the Israelites seem to say, "It was the LORD who nearly wiped out Benjamin. And here we are, trying our best to remedy the situation by slaughtering the inhabitants of Jabesh-Gilead and kidnapping the young women of Shiloh." Truly, by the end of the book, we, the readers of Judges, have witnessed how far Israel has come in confusing what is "evil in the eyes of the LORD" and "what is right in their own eyes." Here, at the end, there are no longer enemies or heroes, oppressors or judges, kings or deliverers. There is just Israel, fully intent on faithlessly, wantonly destroying itself.

 We Have Seen the Enemy: A Cautionary Tale

So what are we to make of this tragic tale of Israel's downfall? What message does it have for us, a message that we might need to hear precisely because we do not want to hear it at all? What part does an art form like "tragedy" have to play in helping us better understand God, ourselves, and our responsibilities toward each other? Can a story with so much violence, so much heartbreak, and at times so much absurdity say anything to us about who we are? Can we hear this tragic story in all its fullness and, at the end, say "This is the Word of the Lord," and hear the response, "Thanks be to God"?

I think we can. Tragedy in general provides us a way of understanding human nature better, a human nature in which choices and decisions can have devastating effects. Simply because we live in a grace-filled relationship with God does not mean that we have no responsibilities either to God or to others. Nor does it mean that when we fail to live up to those responsibilities, our failures and omissions really don't matter. Whatever the Christian message is, and however we may interpret it, that is a wrongheaded way to understand it.

No, as the Confession of Sin in the Book of Common Prayer puts it, "what we have done and what we have left undone" often has serious consequences both for ourselves and for those with whom we live. And, furthermore, when a group of us—a family, a community, a city, an area, or a country—align ourselves together and participate in harmful ways of living, the results can be catastrophic. We must, therefore, be aware of the ways in which we all participate in modes of living that cause ourselves and others harm, and sometimes death.

And that's where an art form like tragedy might help us.

Throughout human history, tragedy provides us with a way to think seriously about who we are and what we do. In this way the book of Judges may serve as a cautionary tale, a warning to pay attention to details that we may too easily overlook in our individual and collective lives. It can function as an excellent resource for helping us to think through some of those unhelpful and harmful ways of living that may be "right on our own eyes," as they were in the eyes of the Israelites under the judges, but at the end of the day are "evil in the eyes of the LORD." It seems to me that there are two prevailing approaches to the book as a whole with relevance for the way we think about our lives, as well as three major themes found throughout Judges that speak directly to the overall message that the book might have for us. These approaches and themes are at the center of the relationship that Israel has with God, with its enemies and oppressors, and with itself. They are, in short, part of what the book is about.

> Judges can be an excellent resource for helping us to think through some of those unhelpful and harmful ways of living that may be "right on our own eyes."

Approach 1: Life Is a Staircase

Several times throughout this book, I have mentioned how the overall shape of the plot of Judges is like a downward slide, in which Israel descends from harmony and happiness and success all the way down to a state of discord, misery, and disaster. This slow movement down the slide, presented in the first introduction, is found in every chapter, as Israel continues to be unfaithful to God and its leaders steadily deteriorate from the time of Ehud onward. This progression, or rather regression, is traced throughout the book as a whole and is part and parcel of every plot of every tragedy that we are familiar with. Thus the book as a whole can be thought of as a gradual descent into chaos.

Here, in the final chapter however, I want to revise that image. The metaphor of a downward slide gives the impression that what happens to Israel throughout the book is unfortunate, certainly, but at the end of the day it is simply what happens. Even as a child naturally careens down a snowy hillside on a sled, or a mass of rocks and earth naturally shifts down a mountain after a torrential rain, so Israel could be thought of as merely unfortunate, losing its claim on happiness and winding up in absolute chaos. Such a movement is disastrous, but sometimes that is just what happens. Israel is just unlucky.

But the book of Judges will not allow us this type of interpretation. In one sense, Israel never chooses to destroy itself, its own tribes and its own people. Viewed in a different light, however, does Israel ever choose to do anything else? Israel, the main character in the tragedy, never chooses anything except that downward path to violence and turmoil. Every scene, every conversation, every action—by Israel as a whole, by its tribes, and by its judges and deliverers—is another step down. Yes, occasionally the Israelites weep for their plight and seem to be sorry and repent of their unfaithfulness. But, unwaveringly, within just a few verses, they are again taking another step away from the peace and harmony they experienced at the beginning of chapter 1 and toward the brutality and violence of chapter 21. For this reason, I would like to suggest that the plot of Judges is not a downward slide, but a descending staircase.

To understand this image, consider the many different ways we think of our own lives. I suspect that many, if not most, of us think of our lives as much of the same day-to-day routine that is occasionally blessed with a few truly wonderful events and interrupted by a few truly awful ones. For example, when we think back over our lives, we remember that first date, or the birth of a child, or when we landed that perfect job, or that party when we celebrated that milestone birthday or anniversary. Or we remember the death of someone important to us, or the time we lost that perfect job, or when the diagnosis came

The plot of Judges is not a downward slide, but a descending staircase.

back with bad news. When we think about our lives, in other words, we think about those times and places we made certain decisions that changed the course of our future. Our memory of our lives revolves around certain, particular events that have happened in the course of a rather humdrum, constant, day-to-day existence.

But Judges witnesses to another approach and another way of understanding life. You see, the essence of Judges is not the story of Israel's deliverance by the judges, nor about Ehud's stabbing of Eglon or Jael's nailing Sisera's head to the ground. It is not about Gideon's troops breaking the pots and showing their torches and confusing the enemy, or Jephthah's victory, or even about Samson pulling the building down upon himself and the Philistines gathering there to celebrate. Nor is it simply about the more ignominious events, such as Barak's reluctance to confront the enemy, Gideon's cowardice, Abimelech's killing of his brothers, or Jephthah's sacrifice of his daughter, or Samson's falling asleep with his head in Delilah's lap. No, the book is not about certain stories or scenes, here and there. Rather the unfolding of the plot of Judges is single, unified, and inexorable. Every chapter contributes to the whole; every scene and every conversation has a role and a part to play in the story. In this tragedy every paragraph and every verse is another step willfully and deliberately taken down that staircase that leads from life to death.

Our lives, Judges attests, are just like that. The direction that we are going, both individually and collectively, is not determined by those big events, whether they be good or bad. The direction we are going is determined by where we are stepping here, right now, today. And then tomorrow. And then the next day. And we are either walking up that staircase or we are walking down it. Judges, it seems to me, shows us readers what happens when we decide that walking down is the best direction to go.

Approach 2: Life Is a Series of Cycles

While the plot of Judges and of our lives can be thought of as a staircase, that is not the only way that the book is organized. The second introduction to the book lays out a pattern that will be played out—

more or less—throughout the central section of judge/deliverer stories: sin, oppression, deliverance, peace, and then sin again. This regular pattern is one of the clearest and most definable characteristics of the book. In almost any commentary on the book of Judges that you might consult from almost any perspective or outlook, practically all of them will recognize that the book is "episodic." That is, the book is organized according to a series of separate and easily defined episodes, each of which have a judge or deliverer as a main character that focuses the plot.

As such, this pattern is reflected in our own lives as well. Even my use of the phrase "day-to-day" to describe the non-eventful portion of our lives signals this way of understanding ourselves. Our lives follow certain predictable patterns. Each life is organized according to separate episodes, whether we think about those in terms of daily events, or seasons, or work schedules, or places and times of where we live, or larger stretches like childhood, young adulthood, adulthood, middle age, old age. If we think about our lives in terms of our "life story" or the "plot of our lives," that plot or that story often involves episodes, times that are bound together to form a smaller unit within the larger whole of our lives.

And while there is a certain cyclical pattern to our lives, it is also clear that no two patterns are identical. Although we may think of our days, particularly throughout the working week, as being made up of the same exact elements (wake up, get dressed, go to work, work, come home from work, relax, sleep, wake up), in fact, no two days are identical. The fact that our lives are episodic means that while there is a regular pattern to them, there is change as well.

In this way, the book of Judges parallels everyone's life. We all live episodically.

The book of Judges, however, is also a tragedy. Part of its tragic plot is not simply that Israel moves from a state of peace and cooperation to a state of violence and chaos. Part of the plot mechanism is the fact that those regular patterns in which Israel participates, particularly the regular return to sin, cause not only the descent down the staircase toward disorder, but also slowly tear apart the pattern itself. After Othniel, every turn of the cycle not only introduces another situation and another deliverer, but also introduces another complication to the cycle itself.

- With Ehud, Israel appears to sin even before he dies at the end of the cycle.
- With Deborah and Barak (and Jael), God never actually raises up a deliverer within the story.
- With Gideon, he himself actually causes Israel to sin at the end of the cycle.
- With Abimelech, the cycle folds in on itself and focuses on the oppressor rather than the deliverer.
- With Jephthah, the destruction of the oppressor is only a prelude to his destruction of his daughter and other Israelite tribes.
- With Samson, the cycle is practically non-existent because he looks more like a Philistine than an Israelite.

Throughout the book of Judges, the disappearance of the pattern parallels the worsening quality of the deliverers and the decay of Israel itself. Eventually, the pattern disappears and the conclusions tell the story of a people whose only desire is to do "what is right in their own eyes."

I think there are also ways in which we as individuals, communities, and nations today can act and participate in ways of living that destroy the order and pattern of people's lives, including our own. Sometimes, looking at our daily or yearly activities can give us an indication of, to use Jesus' words, "where our heart is" (Mark 6:21; Luke 12:34). What do those regular patterns of our lives tell us about how we live and what is most important to us? Do they bring about peace and harmony both for ourselves and for others, or do they cause confusion, anger, frustration, or hatred? Do those patterns have a tendency, like the book of Judges, to self-destruct and lead toward more chaos? Our lives are organized according to a series of patterns—that much is true. But are those patterns bringing about a larger plot that leads closer and more toward life or toward death? Judges, it seems to me, shows us readers what happens when we choose to live according to

The disappearance of the regular pattern of sin, deliverance, and rest parallels the worsening quality of the judges and the decay of Israel itself.

the unhelpful and destructive patterns of behavior in our lives and in the lives around us.

In this way looking at Judges as a whole story, from beginning to ending, provides us with a mirror in which we can see ourselves and how we live, move, and have our being. Our lives are like walking on a staircase, either up or down. Our lives are also like a series of cycles or episodes, which lead to life and peace or death and chaos. Judges, both overall and through its stories, provides us with a way of thinking about ourselves, in Aristotle's words "arousing pity and fear," while simultaneously helping us to deal with our own flaws and weaknesses.

Apart from this overarching way of thinking about Judges and our lives, there are also a few consistent themes within the book that can contribute to a "conversation with Scripture" that we might have, both alone with the text and in the company of others. There are, no doubt, dozens of ways that the stories of Judges reflect or reverberate or refract our understanding of ourselves, but here are three that have stood out to me while I've been writing this book. As I reflect upon each of them, I will mention some of the questions that these issues bring up for me in light of the book of Judges and in light of my own life. Since part of the purpose of this series is to spur "conversations," I hope that you might take my questions and suggestions to heart and, perhaps, have conversations with your own fellow travelers on this journey.

Sin as Addiction

The topic of sin is one that makes many Christians, particularly many Episcopalians and Anglicans, uncomfortable. In her remarkable little book, *Speaking of Sin: The Lost Language of Salvation*, Barbara Brown Taylor notes that many churches have foregone the confession of sin in their Sunday morning liturgies in order that worship may become a more "positive experience." She notes, however, that this is a serious error because the basic Christian affirmation is two-fold: God redeems the world from its sin through the cross of Christ, and we are to participate in that redemption. If we ignore sin, thinking that it is simply an out-moded and archaic concept—like the circles of hell or multiple angels dancing on the heads of pins—then we come close to forfeiting our real participation in God's work. It is more comfortable for us to believe that God forgives us our sins, than it is to believe that God supports us to quit them. "But," she asks, "how can we quit them if we have forgotten what they are called?"

> Before he was welcomed home, the prodigal son "came to." He recognized his sin against his father. He prepared his confession. He left one way of life for another, ready to do penance when he arrived home. His father's kiss erased it all, but not because the son was innocent. The son was guilty and he knew it, which is what gave the kiss its power. Jesus' own kiss comes to us in the form of a cross. If we remain unaware of our collusion with the forces of death that put him there, then it will be very difficult for us to receive his absolution, with its stunning offer of new life.[15]

For the present age, sin retains its power mostly from our unwillingness to acknowledge it. But this will not do if we are to take the book of Judges seriously.

If one thinks that "sin" is equated with minor slips and insignificant indulgences, then the narrative of Judges will appear to be a series of unfortunate events. If the constant refrain "Then Israel again did what was evil in the eyes of the LORD" is equated with moral lapses or an occasional giving into temptation, the overall story will not make sense. If the worship of Baal and Asherah is translated into contemporary language as something like "doing something wrong" or "messing up," then, I fear, we may miss the whole point of the story.

For "sin" in the book of Judges appears much less like Israel doing certain illicit actions and more like a constant addiction to a damaged and damaging way of life. If we think of addiction in the life of an individual, whether it be an addiction to alcohol or drugs or abusive sexual activity, I think all of us can appreciate the way that such a lifestyle is deadly. The recurring obsession with a particular substance or activity becomes the center of the person's life, undermining all other relationships and all other responsibilities. If we could multiply this addictive behavior, so that an entire society becomes so obsessed with the object it desires, then we can begin to understand

what Judges means when it says that "Israel did
what was evil in the sight of the LORD."

As it is portrayed in the book of Judges, Israel
is a society that seems obsessed with turning away
from a exclusive relationship with its God. From
the cyclical pattern introduced in the second
introduction of the book, through the beginning of the stories of
Othniel, Ehud, Deborah, and Barak, whenever Israel was left on its
own without a leader, it turned immediately away from the worship of God to something else. With the deliverance of Gideon,
however, the addictive sin of Israel becomes more complex. Gideon
himself sets up illicit objects of worship in his own hometown,
which causes both Israel to become unfaithful and his own family
to become ensnared. Gideon, the one called by God to help Israel
and deliver Israel, becomes an enabler of Israel's addiction, of
Israel's unfaithfulness.

> Through its stories Judges
> gives us a way of thinking per-
> ceptively about ourselves and
> helping us to deal with our
> own flaws and weaknesses.

The compulsiveness of Israel is next illustrated in the reign of
Abimelech, Gideon's son. Funded through resources taken from the
temple of Baal-Berith, Abimelech conspires, manipulates, and forces
himself upon Israel, with disastrous consequences. In the story of
Abimelech, the deadly addiction of Israel's faithlessness comes home
in the leadership of Israel itself. With Jephthah, furthermore, we see
the obsession of Israel increase under a leader who attempts to deal
and compromise with Israel's explicit enemies. This in itself may not
be wholly negative, but it is combined with a death-dealing attitude
toward those in his own family and a sense of warring vengeance
against others within Israel. In the tale of Jephthah, we see the fractured nature of a leader who does not respond justly to his enemies,
his family, or his allies.

With Samson, this addictive faithlessness comes full circle in a
leader who looks, essentially, like a Philistine. Although he was called
to be a Nazarite, a faithful leader completely devoted to God, and a
deliverer for Israel, Samson almost immediately turns away from his
vow and spends his entire life enmeshed in Philistine society. While
in his death he kills more Philistines than he does during his life, he
kills them—in his own words—to wreak vengeance upon them for
blinding him. Samson, as a symbol of the faithlessness of Israel,

wastes his entire life in foolishness and amorous adventures. His story is the longest, but also the most meaningless from the perspective of being a deliverer of Israel.

The final chapters, furthermore, illustrate even more clearly Israel's destructive behavior. Minor incidents, such as Micah's stealing of silver from his mother and the spat between the Levite and his concubine, erupt into full-scale destruction. The viciousness and deadliness of Israel's continual return to sinful behavior have no remedy in these episodes. Near the end of the book, we are told about a little town called Laish, which is easily destroyed by a band of renegades because it had no deliverer. Israel, like the city of Laish, has no deliverer by the end of the book. No Othniel, no Ehud, no Jeththah, not even a Samson. Israel finally earns the goal toward which it continually strives throughout the whole book: an existence where it can "follow its own way," regardless of whether it is good or evil.

The book of Judges will not allow us to think of sin as minor gaffes and improprieties. No, "sin" for this book is essentially found in the concept of addictive idolatry. Israel cannot seem to escape its constant obsession with turning to foreign deities for its identity and security. For whatever reason, the Israelites have become psychologically, socially, and theologically dependent not upon the LORD, the God of Israel, but with the gods of their Canaanite neighbors.

What are those obsessions that we have that we use to define ourselves besides our central relationship with our own true and mysterious God? What are those things that we rely upon to give us our worth and identity? How do we express our complete and utter obsession with them? How is this like (or unlike) Israel's obsession with "the Baals and Asherahs" of Canaan? Can we discern any warnings from the text that might speak to our own obsessions, to whatever makes us weak and dependent on things that cannot help or save?

Violence and Peace

Anyone who gives Judges even a casual reading cannot but notice that violence is a constant motif throughout the book. From the very first scene all the way through to the last, Israel finds itself in turmoil. The way that violence and peace are portrayed is not consistent throughout the book, however. Because of Israel's compulsive tendency to turn away from God at every opportunity, the violence of its society becomes more and more pronounced. Consequently violence progresses from being a "by-product" of living in a war-ridden time and area, to becoming the warp and woof of their lives as a whole.

Israel cannot seem to escape its constant obsession with turning to foreign deities for its identity and security.

In the introductions, war and violence are merely mentioned as the background of the story; they are not the point. When Israel wins a battle, or, conversely, loses a battle, the point is the win or the loss. We are told little of the number of those who died; violence is the subtext of these initial stories. Also, in the story of Othniel, there is little in the way of carnage; his victory over Cushan-Rishataim is quick and seemingly bloodless. While we all know that there is no such thing as a "bloodless war," the violence of war is not the focus of these early stories. Judges, when it begins, is not a book of "gratuitous violence."

With both of the victories of Ehud and of Deborah and Barak, the violence is vivid, but is directed against an individual enemy. We see no bloodshed during the wars with either the Moabites or the Canaanites. Israel seems to win the wars with few losses, while the enemy's fallen are neither described nor highlighted.

Similarly, in the time of Gideon this pattern continues. Israel seems to win its battle against the Midianites by having the enemy kill themselves in a panic, so their job is only to pursue the few who escape their comrades' swords and track them down. A change occurs, however, in the story when Gideon vows vengeance upon the towns of Succoth and Penuel, who are fellow Israelites. Because the inhabitants of these towns are suspicious of Gideon's military ability, they withhold giving him food for his journey. After Gideon successfully tracks down the kings of Midian, he turns his troops against the Israelite towns and tortures those who dwell in them. For the first time, violence erupts against Israelites by Israelites. And the violence that erupts becomes a part of the plot of the story just as much as the inhabitants of the towns or of Gideon himself. Thus the story is no longer about sin, oppression, or deliverance, but has escalated to violent abuse and torture. This is an important, and tragic, change in the quality of the book as a whole. This inter-Israelite violence, of course, flourishes in the story of Abimelech and his slaughter of his own family, his own hometown, and the neighboring city of Thebez. And the violence that Abimelech instigates eventually comes to rest upon his own head, in the form of a millstone dropped from a great height.

Jephthah's war against the enemy, the Ammonites, is practically bloodless. This might lead us to think that finally—finally—the story might be changing away from violence and torture. But when he arrives home, Jephthah brings about his own daughter's death with an air of righteous superiority and, like Gideon, launches his own war against fellow Israelites, in this case the tribe of Ephraim. Yet, unlike Gideon, Jephthah attempts an all-out extermination, savagely hunting down individual Ephraimites who attempt to escape.

Surprisingly, the story of Samson has little comparable violence; the minor tricks and the few skirmishes Samson brings about are only an indication of his own futility as a deliverer. So little violence appears in the Samson story because Samson does not associate with Israelites at all and his associations with the Philistines are mostly fraternizing, if not exactly friendly. The violent reactions of the Philistines themselves is highlighted in the burning of Samson's wife and her family, but this is mentioned in a single verse. When Samson does bring about a full-scale slaughter, it occurs in a single verse. His death and accompanying destruction of Philistines in the last moments of his life are lightly passed over.

By the time we arrive at the concluding chapters, things are much different, and the violence that has been suppressed during the somewhat fatuous life of Samson erupts. Violence is widespread and described in detail. The destruction of Laish is accompanied by the mention in two separate passages that the city dwelled in peace, a sympathetic perspective that only heightens the tragedy of its destruction. But this scene pales in comparison with the horrific scenes in the final ending: from the butchery of the Levite's concubine to the seemingly unending battle waged against the Benjaminites to the horrific consequences of the war, these scenes of the book turn our attention fully toward the violence that has become the point of the story. By the end of the book, violence has become no longer simply the unfortunate by-product of the price of Israel's security, but rather the whole of its social life.

As the book progresses through its story, its violence grows exponentially to take center stage. It is as if this minor element grows first into a pattern, then into an occasional motif, then into a larger theme, then, finally, it swallows the plot and becomes the point of the story itself. I suspect this slow, almost imperceptible spread of violence is not just a literary technique that appears in Judges, but also part of the character of violence itself. It is amazing to me how inured human beings can become to violence in television or movies or music when it is fed to us a little at a time.

> The slow, almost imperceptible spread of violence is not just a literary technique in Judges, but also part of the nature of violence itself.

What is our own attitude toward violence? How is violence manifested in our common life together? Is it something that we deplore, or do we acknowledge it as inevitable? Is it something that we see as sometimes (or even oftentimes) as necessary and good?

Do we see any "progression" in the violence of our world or in the violence that we endure or perpetrate? How does violence grow? Are we becoming more violent, or less violent? Does violence always take the form of war, or slaughtered children, or abused spouses? Or does violence take other forms, more subtle or less easily seen or recognized forms, either for us or within the book of Judges itself? Do either of these give insight into the other?

"Us Versus Them"

As we have seen before, sometimes themes are not merely topics or situations that occur regularly throughout a story. Sometimes a theme might involve something that is not consistent, or it could be signaled by a change that occurs throughout a book. This is particularly true, I believe, of the way that enemies are portrayed in the book of Judges.

At the beginning of the judge cycle, the enemy of Israel is personalized—for example, when Israel disobeys, its people are sold into the hand of a single individual, Cushan-Rishataim. Likewise, when

Othniel wins the deliverance of Israel, the victory involves simply defeating the foreign king:

> The Israelites did what was evil in the sight of the LORD, forgetting the LORD their God, and worshiping the Baals and the Asherahs. Therefore the anger of the LORD was kindled against Israel, and he sold them into the hand of King Cushan-rishathaim of Aram-naharaim; and the Israelites served Cushan-rishathaim eight years. But when the Israelites cried out to the LORD, the LORD raised up a deliverer for the Israelites, who delivered them, Othniel son of Kenaz, Caleb's younger brother. The spirit of the LORD came upon him, and he judged Israel; he went out to war, and the LORD gave King Cushan-rishathaim of Aram into his hand; and his hand prevailed over Cushan-rishathaim (3:7–10).

Notice how often the king's name appears. This is definitely an individual, a person. After this throughout the book, however, the enemy of Israel becomes both more complex and less individualized.

With Ehud, God sells Israel into the hand of King Eglon of Moab. But Ehud's killing of King Eglon does not win the victory, for he must still fight against Israel's real enemy, the Moabites themselves. Deliverance is finally won, not by the killing of the human King Eglon, but the victory over the faceless "Moabites." Likewise, with Deborah and Barak, the oppressor is not only King Jabin of Hazor, but also his general, Sisera. Thus deliverance is won not only by the routing of the army of Sisera, but by Sisera himself. In this case, King Jabin is not the point of either oppression or deliverance at all.

The story of Gideon marks a major extension of this theme. When the Israelites sin, they are sold into the hand of the nameless, faceless hordes of "Midian," as well as "the Amalekites." When victory is won, however, it involves not only the routing of the army of Midian, but also the beheading of the generals of the army, Oreb and Zeeb, and the killing of the two kings of Midian, Zebah and Zalmunna. With the story of Abimelech the portrayal of the "enemy" reaches a true turning point. The enemy throughout the story is Abimelech himself, an Israelite. The Israelite enemy lies at the heart of this story. After this point in the book, however, when non-Israelite enemies are portrayed they are almost always nameless and faceless entities. In the Jephthah story, the enemy is simply described as "the

Ammonites" and "the Philistines," with no real flesh-and-blood Ammonite or Philistine mentioned by name. Although Jephthah tries to negotiate with their leader, the text never gives him a name; he is, simply, "the king of the Ammonites." Moreover, when Jephthah wins deliverance for Israel, his victory is over "the Ammonites." After the war against the Ammonites, Jephthah again fights against people who confront him. In this case, the text calls them simply the "men of Ephraim" or, simply, "Ephraim."

Throughout the Samson stories the enemy is described simply as "the Philistines." When individual Philistines are portrayed, moreover, they are almost never named, but are simply called "a woman of Timnah" or "the young men," "Samson's wife," "her father," "the men of the town," "a prostitute," or "the lords of the Philistines." The one exception to this is, of course, the anti-hero of the story, Delilah. But by this point in the story Samson is no longer the deliverer of Israel, but has become the "oppressor" of Philistia. Because of his close identification with the Philistines, the story has essentially become one describing the defeat of the enemy of the Philistines (that is, Samson himself), rather than the story of the deliverer of Israel. As such, the Philistine deliverer—in a sense, the Philistine "judge" who wins the day—is Delilah herself. Judges slowly evolves from stories of individual judges and warriors to being about anonymous and hostile masses. In the end, this is how Israel views itself.

Judges slowly evolves from stories of individual judges and warriors to being about anonymous and hostile masses. In the end, this is how Israel views itself.

In the concluding chapters of Judges, the enemies of Israel are similarly impersonal: the inhabitants of the city of Laish, the men of Gibeah, the Benjaminites. There is, moveover, one additional enemy that is also generically described, and it is "Israel" itself. By the end of the story we no longer see the enemies of Israel as individual warriors, and we also see Israel itself as a nameless, faceless entity. The book has slowly moved from being about individual people to objectified masses of humanity. In the end, this is how Israel views itself— not individual tribes or characters with real faces and names.

At this point, I think, the teaching of Judges is very subtle and insightful. As I read through the story from the introductions through the judge stories of deliverance to the conclusions, I am, in a sense, sucked into the perspective of Israel itself. As readers, we are lulled into seeing the enemies of Israel in less and less human ways. Is this what the book actually wants us to do, to see our enemies as a nameless and faceless "them"? Or does it, perhaps, want us to reflect on the story as a whole, as a tragedy, and ask whether, perhaps, this tendency of Israel itself, as it is reflected in the plot of the story, is actually at the heart of the tragic flaw of Israel.

When I reflect on the question of the teaching of Judges as a whole, I wonder if there is, in fact, a danger in even using the term "they" or "them" to describe those people, those individuals, who would seek to do us harm? And if there is a danger in this, is the reverse also true? Is there an equal danger in lumping everyone who agrees with me as some great, nameless, faceless "us"? Do we only know who "we" are by referring to "them"? Conversely, do we only know of "them" because they are not "us"? Does the tendency to depersonalize "them" often spill over into a depersonalization of "us" ourselves? Moreover, the areas and boundaries of the definition of who "we" are can change. "We" can be defined as general humanity, or by a particular nation or society, or a certain region, or a particular church or denomination or congregation. In other words, the questions are about "us," but this can be asked from any number of perspectives. Who *are* "we" anyway? These are questions that must be asked time and again.

There is, of course, more to be said. There are more lessons to be learned and more questions that can be raised than the few that I've highlighted here. Anyone who comes to the end of reading a biblical book and thinks, "Well, now I know what that is about," has missed both the point of the book and the point of reading the Bible to begin with. These are texts that never end. These are texts that are living, and powerful, and can reach deep inside us. Are there other ways to read Judges? Absolutely. Are there other questions that the text raises for us? No doubt. But these few approaches and themes, I hope, might provide you a way to start thinking theologically about this often overlooked book.

By using the text of Judges to gain a hold and a perspective on the various questions that it raises, we are constantly driven anew to the text, and then back to ourselves, redefining in each case what the book is saying and teaching and who we are now and who we might become. The book of Judges becomes, in this way, no longer only an object that we study. It becomes also a subject that studies us, that defines us, that urges us on to a better, and deeper, and wider understanding of who we are and what we are doing here, as well as a more mature insight into the God in whom we live and move and have our being.

ACKNOWLEDGMENTS

While it may be true that my name appears on the cover of this book, I am merely the author. Whatever is good and honest and true within this book comes from so many sources and so many people that to mention them all would require an acknowledgement that is longer than this book itself. Here, I can only point out a few people who have helped me put these few ideas down on paper so that you can read them.

I want to thank my mentors at Yale, Robert Wilson and Ellen Davis, who showed me that a critical and careful understanding of the Bible did not exclude an awareness of its power and its ability to change our lives for the better. Like the disciples on the road to Emmaus, I remember so many times during my graduate career how my "heart burned" within me while these scholars and friends opened the scriptures, both in their classes as well as in their lives.

Thanks are also due to my colleague, Fred Schmidt, who asked me one day while we were walking from our cars, "Roy, would you be willing to write a volume in the Conversations with Scripture series that I edit?" Because of Fred's encouragement and care during the subsequent couple of years, I was able to see this book come into being.

Writing a book takes time. I thank Dean William Lawrence and the Perkins School of Theology at SMU for the generous research leave benefits that it extends to its faculty. The initial draft of this book was drawn up during the spring of 2009 during my leave from classes. Without the space to think and research and write, I doubt this book would have seen the light of day.

I also need to thank various colleagues and friends who have heard, read, marked, learned, and otherwise inwardly digested various versions of this book or parts of this book: Carolyn Sharp, Rich Nelson, Serge Frolov, Stephen Riley, Cheryl Strimple, Robert Foster, Jouette Bassler, Kai Ryan, and Tim Ryan. Thank you all for listening patiently while I blathered on about cycles and spirals and tragedy and deliverer stories. Your listening made this a better book.

I want to express my profound gratitude to Cynthia Shattuck, the editor for this book. She is a true alchemist, taking what was leaden and gray and transforming it into something that is clear and golden. Her questions and suggestions for revision were always right on target. This book is much, much stronger and richer because she had a hand in it.

An eternal debt is also due to those people who have made me who I am at a very personal level. My parents, Velma and Louis Heller, my wife, Amy, and my children, Noah and Annie, have all contributed to this book by making its author a better person than he has any right to be. I love you all.

Writing a book for a general readership is a very difficult thing. So many questions arise: What do people know about the Bible? What do they expect from a book like this? What do they most need to understand and take away from reading it? My in-laws, Barb and Don Groves, have been a constant source of joy and wisdom during the past eighteen years of our knowing one another. Their commitment to faith and the church, their willingness to ask and to learn, and their awareness of what is most important in life have been a model of what it means to be "an educated layperson." For these reasons, I dedicate this volume to them.

STUDY QUESTIONS

by Sharon Ely Pearson

The book of Judges continues the story of the people of Israel from the death of Joshua (Judges 2:8) to just before the birth of Samuel (1 Samuel 1). After an incomplete conquest that leaves much in the hands of Israel's foes, Israel's life in the land follows a recurring pattern of disloyalty to God followed by oppression by enemies. Many of these stories are the stuff of which Hollywood has captured on the big screen, notably Samson and Delilah, Gideon, and Deborah. They are the larger-than-life characters of Sunday school classrooms of long ago. Roy Heller engages us in reading the stories of these so-called judges—sometimes military leaders and oftentimes flawed champions—in new ways. For many of you, this may be the first time you read Judges as a whole and will discover a very different set of stories than those of childhood memories. They are stories of violence, blood, destruction, and death. Not always what we have remembered. And our heroes are not seen in the most positive of lights—in God's eyes or the readers.

Over and over again we will read stories of tribal heroes who continually fall into a downward spiral of sin. One might also see parallels in our own lives, communities, and the world today. As Heller states, "Judges may not be the happiest book in the Bible, but it is certainly one of the most artful and beautifully written. I believe its message in one of the most important for those who are dealing with community, particularly broken community, and are seeking a way of thinking about what it means to live in community more fully." May we come to see how these tribal stories connect to our relationship to God and one another in the twenty-first century.

Introduction

This study guide is meant to accompany each chapter as a path to go deeper and reflect upon the events, personalities and ideas that the author unpacks through the chapters of Judges. The questions and reflections will invite you into a conversation about the role of these stories that have been passed down through the generations—of the Hebrew people and us today. How we connect with the theological themes and motifs in these stories of Yahweh's deliverance of Israel can have significance to our own relationships and spiritual lives.

The book of Judges follows the book of Joshua and purports to cover the history of Israel from the time of the settlement in Canaan until just before the establishment of the monarchy. These are stories and legends of Israel's time of tribal life in Palestine, from approximately 1250 to 1050 BCE. The book presents the subjects of its narratives as referring to all of Israel when originally these figures were associated with particular tribes. The exploits of twelve judges are followed, six of them ("Minor Judges": Shamgar, Tola, Jair, Ibzan, Elon, and Abdon) are hardly mentioned except by a single incident. The other six ("Major Judges": Othniel, Ehud, Barak with Deborah, Gideon, Jephthah, and Samson) were renowned for their brave exploits in battle and were not really legal judges but warlords. In the face of Israel's faithlessness and consequent disaster, Yahweh repeatedly provides her with charismatic leaders. So, we have come to understand the book of Judges as a collection of stories about ancient tribal heroes, as well as symbolic of Israel as a whole.

As you begin this study of Judges, consider the following:

- Why are you engaging in this study of the book of Judges?
- What have your previous understandings of this period of time in Israel's life been? Do you go into this study with any preconceived notions? If so, jot them down before reading.
- What do you hope to learn and discern for yourself in this study?
- What was the world like at this period of our world's history? How is it different to today's world? Similar?

Before studying each chapter of this book, portions of Scripture may be suggested to read ahead of time. You may also wish to have a map of the Tribes of Israel in Canaan. These can be found in the appendix of most study bibles. As you read Judges, look at the significant places on the map and note what happened there.

Chapter One: The Book of Judges as Tragedy

The first chapter begins with Heller's own relationship with Judges. He believes the church has not largely dealt with—or known—the book of Judges as a whole. Begin by reflecting on your own relationship with Judges:

- When you hear the "book of Judges," what stories, if any, from childhood to you remember?
- What was the context from which your memory comes? Church? Sunday school? Home? A children's bible? The movies? A sermon?
- What is your understanding of who the "judges" were in the biblical history of the Hebrew Scriptures?
- What is a judge?

Heller reviews how the book of Judges has been considered throughout Christian history. He notes that is has not been considered "theological" or "spiritual" and was often overlooked by preachers and teachers. One of Heller's questions is, "How can a violent, blood-soaked narrative of morally ambiguous characters be read spiritually, devotional, or theologically?" Before opening to Judges 1:1 to begin our study, consider the following:

- What makes a text or story theological?
- What makes a text or story spiritual?
- Do you believe Judges is a theological or spiritual text? Why or why not? Give examples.
- Throughout Christian history, what did it mean to be a judge? How is this similar or different in our communities today? In the world?
- Why would Yahweh (God) continually provide charismatic leaders to Israel? Does God provide such leaders today?
- What is justice?

Due to the violent nature of the stories of Judges, we are invited to view this book as a tragedy by Heller. He shares, "Tragedies have a great deal to tell us about what it means to be human" and "Because tragedies function to warn us of the dramatic consequences of the flaws to which we are all liable, we often would rather ignore their warnings or try to rationalize or gloss over them."

- How does Heller define tragedy?
- How do you define tragedy?
- What tragedies have occurred in your life?
- What tragedies are occurring in our world today?
- Are any of the above related to aspects of our religious and moral life as an individual or society?

Chapter Two: Back When Life Was Simple: The Introductions

We begin reading Judges by understanding there are two different introductions. Heller describes them as "diachronic" and "synchronic." Judges 1:1–2:5 describes the conquest of Canaan as gradual and piecemeal. Instead of a single unified force under Joshua, it is tribal armies that wage battles in various parts of Canaan; going from success to failure. In Judges 2:6–3:6 another motif emerges that presents us with a four-fold pattern: sin > punishment > repentance > deliverance. As we will learn, this pattern is circular and repeated throughout Judges. Heller describes this as a "downward spiral, a 'cycle' in which each successive story descends further down the slope toward chaos."

Read Judges 1:1–2:5 and 2:6–3:6

- Keep a log of the vignettes as you read them, and continue to do so throughout your reading of Judges. How are the patterns of sin, oppression, deliverance, and death of the judge stated in these beginning chapters?
- How does each further descend "down the slope"?
- Is there any particular action that leads to sin in these beginning stories?
- What does it mean to "do evil in the sight of the LORD"?

We begin to get a sense of the violence that is to come throughout Judges. Heller suggests spending some time wrestling with the concept of retribution. He explores a variety of concepts that are different than our twenty-first-century understanding of a mean-spirited, vengeful response to past offenses. Discuss your understanding of the following:

- *Shillam*
- *Shalom*
- *Karma*
- Peace
- Justice
- Betrayal
- Loyalty
- Success

In the coming chapters of Judges we will again and again read of Israel's sin.

How does the editor of Judges (the Deuteronomist) have us understand the meaning of sin to be?

- What is Heller's definition?
- How is either of these different or similar to your own understanding of sin?
- Using the same three questions above, how would you answer for the definition of evil?

The four-fold pattern of salvation: sin, judgment, repentance, and redemption, is found throughout the book of Judges. The terms are also referred to in the Catechism in the Book of Common Prayer (pages 848–849). Look for examples in history, in our own times, in your own life.

- Why is this a useful model?
- What other models do we have in our culture for dealing with the existence of evil that holds less promise because they do not bring a true sense of redemption?
- How does our penchant for punishment and revenge match up with this Judeo/Christian pattern of salvation?

Chapter Three: Faithfulness and Fickleness: Othniel to Gideon

As we begin to read stories of the twelve judges, note the four-fold pattern for each character. Each begins within a period of apostasy, and Yahweh's "spirit" comes upon a new leader. If possible, read the stories in a variety of translations of the Bible, such as the NRSV, The Message, and the Common Bible.

Read Judges 3:7–8:32a

- What is your reaction to these stories?
- Why do you think Heller believes the story of Othniel is the most important of all the stories of the Judges?
- What does it mean for the land to have "quietude" and "placidity"?
- Compare and contrast the various stories of each of the "major" judges.

Judges 4:1–5:31 Deborah and Barak

Chapters 4 and 5 of Judges give two versions of the Deborah story, a prose account and a poem of song. The song is by far the earlier version. It is the oldest complete narrative song in the Old Testament. The "song of Miriam" (Exodus 15:21) and the "song of the ark" (Numbers 10:35–36) are also ancient, but they are not narratives. *Focus on Judges 5:2–31.*

- How is God described in relationship to the judges past and present?
- Why do you think this ancient song was retained as part of the story of Deborah and Barak?
- How is Deborah different than the previous judges, besides that she is female? Is this of any importance?

By the end of chapter 5, we are "becoming uncomfortably aware that judges are not strictly necessary to bring about deliverance." Heller believes the story of Deborah, Barak, and Jael raises many questions, but leaves us with some also:

- Will God continue to raise up judges? And if so, for what purpose?
- Will they continue to "deliver" Israel? Or will they have another role?
- How might we answer these questions after each of the vignettes? In our world today?

Judges 6:1–8:35 Gideon

Again, the Deuteronomist describes Israel as crying to Yahweh for help in distress, and Yahweh replying with deliverance. We are presented with the call of Gideon as the deliverer of the people. In it a favorite theme of many Israelite storytellers: Yahweh chooses one of the weakest in Israel to confound the might oppressor.

- Who else in scripture does Gideon remind you of?
- How would you describe the character of Gideon?
- Compare Gideon with Moses (Exodus 3) and Aaron (Exodus 32). Where are the similarities? Differences?

Chapter Four: The Downward Spiral: Abimelech to Samson

The story of Abimelech, the half-Israelite, half-Canaanite son of Gideon and his concubine, plots to become king. This story is from Israel's tradition that saw monarchy as a betrayal of Yahweh's sovereignty (see 1 Samuel 8). Heller describes the following stories and their character as "almost comical" and "morally bankrupt warriors." No wonder they were fun to read as children! But they are not funny or role models of what it means to be a leader. Heller calls them "prototypes and representatives of the faithlessness and fickleness of Israel as a whole."

Read Judges 9 Abimelech

The focus of this story is on the oppressor, not the deliverer.

- Why is this story included in Judges?
- Compare Abimelech with his father, Gideon. What is the attitude toward kingship that the stories about Gideon and Abimelech demonstrate?
- What are our attitudes toward the monarchies of today? Are they similar to this period in Israel's time? Why or why not?
- How has the downward spiral escalated from one generation to the next?
- What does this chapter of Judges say to our understanding of systemic oppression today?
- Where does our call for advocating for the oppressed originate?
- Are there stories from current world events in which deliverers become oppressors or oppressors become deliverers? How are

we (personally and corporately) associated with such oppression?

■ What is the moral of the story of Abimelech? Does this pertain to us today?

Read Judges 10:1–12:7 Jephthah

Due to the constant habit of faithlessness, the cyclical pattern of sin, oppression, and deliverance no longer functions to train and discipline Israel to remain faithful. Israel has been delivered into the hands of the Philistines and the Ammonites.

■ How has the spirit of the LORD come upon Jephthah that is different than the previous judges?

■ One of the characteristics that Heller uses to describe Jephthah is that of a "dealer." Where else in Scripture do we see humans negotiating with God or with other people?

■ Do we ever make "deals" with God or our enemies today?

Read Judges 13–16 Samson

Samson is not a judge or even a deliverer in the sense that others mentioned in the book of Judges are. His are tales about a local hero told with no attempt to make them fit into the pattern apostasy, punishment, repentance, and deliverance beyond the opening formula in 13:1 and the closing one in 16:31. For Heller, the stories of Samson are frustrating. He shares many questions, of which you are invited to explore more fully.

■ How would you characterize the stories of Samson? Frustrating? Comedic? Hopeful? Other descriptors?

■ What is symbolic of the theme "spirit of the LORD" through Judges? How has this theme changed? For what purpose has it changed?

■ What does the spirit of God cause people to do in the time of Judges? Today?

■ What is Samson's purpose?

■ If God is God, why does God continue to seek "an opportunity to act" against the oppressor of the Hebrews?

■ What does it mean to be a judge of Israel in the time of Samson?

■ In the time of Samson, words such as "oppression" and "deliverance" have lost all their meaning. When, if any, in our recent history has this been true also?

Chapter Five: Things Fall Apart:
The Conclusions

Through Judges we have been reading the cycle of apostasy, oppression, repentance, and deliverance, followed by new sin again. The conclusion of the Deuteronomistic History states that there is a limit to the infidelity that Yahweh will countenance from Israel before expelling it from the land that had been promised and given to it. It was a time of political, social, and economic disorder. We have read stories in which the "good characters" are also the "bad characters."

Heller begins chapter 5 of his book by telling us, "Biblical characters in stories serve us best when they function like mirrors, giving us the chance to look at them and see ourselves in them—the good parts and bad parts of ourselves together." He uses the movie *High Noon* as a way of thinking about our own sense of justice.

■ What does it mean to be victorious?
■ Are there ever purely "good guys" in stories or in real life?
■ Why doesn't the pattern of sin, deliverance, peace, and renewed sin continue to hold in Judges? Does it exist in our world today? If so, name some examples.
■ When does an oppressor make deliverance necessary?
■ What's the difference between doing right in God's eyes and doing whatever is right in our own eyes?

Read Judges 17–18

The first conclusion is composed of three interconnected stories: the family of Micah and the setting up of an illicit shrine in his home, Micah's hiring of a young Levite to be the priest of his shrine, and the tribe of Dan's destroying the city of Laish. Look at the action of each character in these stories.

■ What does the character do "right in their own eyes"?
■ How is the character oppressed or serve as an oppressor?
■ How does oppression become insidious and intractable during this period?

- How does this pattern repeat itself in our own time?
- How does one know God's absence?
- How do we, the reader of Judges, know what God's opinion is about Micah or about the Danites and their journey?

Heller reviews the theology of what Judges has been describing as we have been reading. "God was helping Israel to live in faithful relationship with themselves and with himself. When Israel failed to live up to their possibilities and slipped into unfaithfulness, God worked to bring them, eventually, back to that faithfulness. The pattern and the theology were for the most part simple and straightforward."

- Refer back to your log on all the judges. What is the purpose of each of their stories from a theological perspective?
- What is your understanding of the purpose of the book of Judges from this first conclusion's perspective?

Read Judges 19–21

By the end of Judges, what is "good in their own eyes" and "what is evil in the eyes of the Lord" has become the same thing. We are faced with some of the most violent passages in the Bible. Assurance of victory has turned into words of judgment. Strength descends to weakness.

- Can God be found in any of these passages?
- How can this story speak theologically even in spite of its bleakness and violent plot? Does it mean something different when considered in light of the previous book or when it is considered by itself?
- In what ways does Israel become the oppressed and the oppressor? How has this been repeated throughout the history of the world?
- How is the character of the nation of Israel different at the conclusion of Judges than it was at its beginning?
  - From strength to weakness . . .
  - From initiative to passivity . . .
  - From life to death . . .
- In your life's experience, where have you seen any of these themes of oppression and judgment?

Chapter Six: We Have Seen the Enemy:
A Cautionary Tale

Our last chapter allows us to reflect on this tragic tale of Israel's downfall. Heller provides numerous questions to challenge our understanding of the book of Judges as well as its implication in our own lives.

- What part does an art form like "tragedy" have to play in helping us better understand God, ourselves and our responsibilities toward each other?
- How does tragedy help us understand human nature more fully?
- What other ways are there to read and understand Judges?

Reflect upon the Confession of Sin from the Book of Common Prayer (p. 360):

Most merciful God,
we confess that we have sinned against you
in thought, word, and deed,
by what we have done,
and by what we have left undone.
We have not loved you with our whole heart;
we have not loved our neighbors as ourselves.
We are truly sorry and we humbly repent.
For the sake of your Son Jesus Christ,
have mercy on us and forgive us;
that we may delight in your will,
and walk in your ways,
to the glory of your Name. Amen.

Heller believes we should "be aware of the ways in which we all participate in modes of living that cause ourselves and others harm, and sometimes death."

- What are the unhelpful and harmful ways of living that may be "right in our own eyes," as they were in the eyes of the Israelites under the judges?
- How is the Confession of Sins the center of our relationship with God?

■ Has the book of Judges impacted your understanding of the Confession of Sins?

There are two approaches to life suggested by Heller in understanding how we can learn from the theological implications of the book of Judges. He states on page 103, "Our lives are like walking on a staircase, either up or down. Our lives are like a series of cycles or episodes, which lead to life and peace or death and chaos. Judges, both overall and through its stories, provides us with a way of thinking about ourselves, in Aristotle's words 'arousing pity and fear,' while simultaneously helping us to deal with our own flaws and weaknesses."

Approach 1: Life Is a Staircase
Approach 2: Life Is a Series of Cycles

■ Which of these approaches most resonant for you?
■ Do you believe our lives follow certain predictable patterns? What examples can you give for your answer?
■ How is your life episodic?
■ What do the regular patterns of our lives tell us about how we live and what is most important to us?
■ Does your life bring about peace and harmony for yourself and for others, or does it cause confusion, anger, frustration, or hatred?
■ Do the patterns have a tendency, like the book of Judges, to self-destruct and lead toward more chaos. If not yourself, do you know anyone with whom this is the pattern of his or her life?
■ How can the patterns of our lives bring us closer to life than toward death?

According to the Catechism in the Book of Common Prayer (p. 848): *Sin is the seeking of our own will instead of the will of god, thus distorting our relationship with God, with other people, and with all creation.*

■ What has sin been in the book of Judges?
■ Do you agree that sin can be an addiction?
■ What are the obsessions that you have that you use to define yourself besides your central relationship with your own true and mysterious God?

- What are those things that you rely upon to give you your worth and identity?
- How do you express your complete and utter obsession with them?
- How might this be like (or unlike) Israel's obsession with "the Baals and Asherahs" of Canaan?
- Can we discern any warnings from the text that might speak to your own obsessions, to whatever makes you weak and dependent on things that cannot help or save?

The slow, almost imperceptible spread of violence in not just a literary technique in Judges, but also part of the nature of violence itself.

- What is your own attitude toward violence?
- How is violence manifested in our common life together?
- Is it something that we deplore, or do we acknowledge it as inevitable?
- Is it something that we see as sometimes (or even oftentimes) as necessary and good?
- Do you see any "progression" in the violence of our world or in the violence that we endure or perpetrate?
- How does violence grow?
- Are we becoming more violent, or less violent?
- What forms does violence take in your life? In your community? In the world?

Concluding thoughts:

- What are the most significant insights you have gleaned from reading the book of Judges?
- How different are you for having engaged in this study?
- What might this book be saying and teaching about who you are today and who you might become in the future?

Sharon Ely Pearson recalls coloring pictures of Gideon blowing the trumpet in Sunday school many years ago as well as being enraptured by a picture of Samson pulling down the temple pillars with his bare hands in her children's illustrated Bible. Today she enjoys equipping others to teach and preach the biblical story to children, youth and adults so that we may become agents of change and reconciliation in a world that often forgets that we are our own worst enemies.

CONTINUING THE CONVERSATION: SUGGESTIONS FOR FURTHER READING

On the early history of the interpretation of Judges, see in particular the recent work by David M. Gunn, *Judges* Blackwell Bible Commentary Series (Malden, MA: Blackwell, 2005). Gunn primarily treats ancient, medieval, early modern, and modern interpretations, with a focus on the way the text has been used practically in religious discussions.

For particular ancient Christian interpretations of passages within Judges, see *Ancient Christian Commentary on Scripture: Vol. IV Joshua, Judges, Ruth, 1–2 Samuel*, ed. John R. Franke (Downer's Grove, IL: InterVarsity, 2005). This work consists mostly of excerpts from the major early Christian writers on biblical interpretation.

A very fine general introduction to Judges can be found at the beginning of the commentary by Susan Niditch, *Judges*, Old Testament Library (Louisville, KY: Westminster John Knox, 2008). It covers the historical background of Judges and deals with the social background of the oral stories in a very accessible way.

Another volume that interprets Judges as a single book having its own integrity is by Barry G. Webb, *The Book of Judges: An Integrated Reading* (Eugene, OR: Wipf & Stock, 1987). Webb's interpretation is based on a very close reading of the text and an awareness how the details of each of the stories contributes to the whole.

One of the ways of dealing with the theological meaning of a biblical book as a whole is to read an appropriate entry in a quality Bible dictionary or one-volume commentary. Because of their length and their purpose, such entries never lose sight of the forest because of the trees. Two such articles are: Lawson G. Stone, "Judges, Book of," in *Dictionary of the Old Testament: Historical Books*, ed. Bill T. Arnold and H. G. M. Williamson (Downers Grove, IL: InterVarsity, 2005), 592–606; and Jerome F. D. Creach, "Judges," in *The New Interpreter's Bible One Volume Commentary*, ed. Beverly Roberts Gaventa and David Petersen (Nashville: Abingdon, 2010), 162–181.

War, violence, and the treatment of women are three prominent issues in the book of Judges that cause most readers discomfort and distress. It is important not to downplay these issues either in the book or in our lives. For scholars who confront these issues in the biblical text head on, see Phyllis Trible, *Texts of Terror: Literary-Feminist Readings of Biblical Narratives* (Philadelphia: Fortress, 1984); Susan Niditch, *War in the Hebrew Bible: A Study in the Ethics of Violence* (New York: Oxford University Press, 1993); Athalya Brenner, ed., *A Feminist Companion to Judges* (Sheffield, England: Sheffield Academic Press, 1999).

Introduction to the Series

1. David F. Ford, "The Bible, the World and the Church I," in *The Official Report of the Lambeth Conference 1998*, ed. J. Mark Dyer et al. (Harrisburg, PA: Morehouse Publishing, 1999), 332.
2. For my broader understanding of authority, I am indebted to Eugene Kennedy and Sara C. Charles, *Authority: The Most Misunderstood Idea in America* (New York: Free Press, 1997).
3. William Sloane Coffin, *Credo* (Louisville, KY: Westminster John Knox Press, 2003), 156.

Chapter One

4. John Chrysostom, *Homilies Concerning the Statutues,* 14.7.
5. Roger Ryan, *Judges: Readings: A New Biblical Commentary* (Sheffield: Sheffield Phoenix, 2007), vii.
6. Aristotle, *Poetics*, trans. Ingram Bywater (New York: Modern Library, 1984), 35.
7. Ruby Cohn, "Tragedy," in *The Cambridge Guide to Theatre* (Cambridge: Cambridge, 1996), 11, 18–20.
8. Jo Ann Hackett, "'There Was No King in Israel': The Era of the Judges" in *The Oxford History of the Biblical World*, ed. Michael D. Coogan (New York: Oxford University Press, 1998), 187–188.

Chapter Two

9. Depending upon what questions a commentator may be asking, other outlines are certainly possible. Other ways of outlining this introduction, as well as the next, may be found in Robert G. Boling, *Judges: Introduction,*

Translation and Commentary, The Anchor Bible (Garden City, NY: Doubleday, 1969), 50–53, 71–74; Michael Wilcock, *The Message of Judges: Grace Abounding* (Downers Grove, IL: InterVarsity, 1992).

Chapter Three

10. Job 3:13, 26; 34:29; 37:17; Ps. 76:9; 83:2; 94:13; Prov. 15:18; Isa. 7:4; 14:7; 18:4; 30:15; 32:17; 57:20; 62:1; Jer. 30:10; 46:27; 47:6f; 48:11; 49:23; Ezek. 16:42, 49; 38:11; Zech. 1:11. Except for Judges, the verb *shaqat* only occurs three times elsewhere in the Deuteronomistic History: Jos. 11:23; 14:15; 2 Kings 11:20.
11. The switching of the death of the judge and the sinning of Israel will eventually be explicit at the end of the Gideon story. There, Gideon actually leads Israel into sin before his death (8:24–27).

Chapter Four

12. Soren Kierkegaard, *Either/Or: A Fragment of Life*, ed. and trans. Howard V. Hong and Edna H. Hong (Princeton, NJ: Princeton University Press, 1987), 30.

Chapter Five

13. Alexander Solzhenitsyn, *The Gulag Archipelago, 1918–1956* (New York: Harper & Row, 1974), 168.
14. As the note in the NRSV acknowledges, the statement "But now I will return it to you" actually occurs at the end of v. 3 in the Hebrew text. It seems clear, however, that it was probably mistakenly copied at that place by a scribe. It makes little sense at the end of v. 3 and makes perfect sense at the end of Micah's speech in v. 2.

Chapter Six

15. Barbara Brown Taylor, *Speaking of Sin: The Lost Language of Salvation* (Cambridge, MA: Cowley, 2000), 4.

ABOUT THE AUTHOR

Roy L. Heller is an Associate Professor of Old Testament at Southern Methodist University's Perkins School of Theology in Dallas. He earned a Ph.D. in Hebrew Bible and Old Testament from Yale University in 1998, and is the author of two books, *Narrative Structure and Discourse Constellations: An Analysis of Clause Function in Biblical Hebrew Prose* and *Power, Politics, and Prophecy: The Character of Samuel and the Deuteronomic Evaluation of Prophecy.* He is particularly interested in the study of Classical Hebrew and in theological and literary interpretations of the Bible. He and his wife, Amy, have two children, Noah and Anne.